What are you searching for?

CW00548914

- Are you are looking for practical ideas and answers that you can put straight into practice over the phone and face-to-face and achieve better results?

- Are you a hunter (new business) or a farmer (account manager) and are looking for tips to generate more business?

- Are you looking for real-life sales tips on all areas of the sales cycle, no matter what products are being sold?

- Are you looking to learn from a real sales expert who has been there and got the tee shirt?

Then this book is for you!

What people are saying about Tony Morris

"We were very impressed with the professionalism and enthusiasm that Tony brought to the table. All our delegates thoroughly enjoyed the training and it is making a huge difference to our business. The creativity, motivation and attention to detail by the trainers transformed a difficult subject into something enjoyable and commercially successful. We will certainly be using Tony again in the future."

Stuart Leckie
Head of sales, Jury's Inn

"We hired Tony in 2008 for sales training and he came up with a course that met our expectations and delivered the results which helped the sales team go from good to great. I would highly recommend Tony for the methods they use, the cost effective nature of their offerings and above all the professionalism which they adopt every step of the way."

Andy Thorne
Business Development Manager, Dukes of London

"We chose Tony and Boyd to train all our lettings negotiators, managers and property management team because of their thorough understanding of our market. They have exceeded all our expectations and we have seen a significant increase in the number of viewings my team make and a massive improvement in their conversions. Their style is innovative, participative and a refreshing change to other training companies we have had in the past. The most important thing to us is that two months later, our people are still using the techniques and we look forward to working with them on a long-term basis."

Dan McCloud & Giles Atkinson
Directors, atkinson mcleod

"I was positively impressed with Tony's approach when training the Oakley London retail team. He kept the team engaged throughout the two days and delivered a course in an enjoyable manner that not only introduced the right tools but also inspired the team to be better. I would recommend Tony to any retail company that wants to improve the organisation's customer service standards, increase their average order value and increase customer retention. We look forward to working with Tony for the foreseeable future."

Paolo Cimbri
Retail Operations Manager, Oakley EMEA

"Tony provided sales training for my team in the Logistics Field, and after just one session, we saw positive results and increased business/ opportunities.

We found Tony's techniques in gaining decision makers a key for our development and continue to work with Tony on a weekly basis, now stretching to over 10 months. I would highly recommend Tony's services in training."

James Hall at UCS

"Tony is the master at what he does. He inspires and delivers in such a way that is refreshing, honest and actually works. Since having my training with Tony, I have continued to use his ideas and out and out costiveness and enthusiasm towards sales and never looked back since. I would highly recommend Tony to any hirer for his thorough and innovative results he achieves."

Sue Mather, Sales Consultant at Top Gear Recruitment

About the Author

Tony Morris was married in 2006 to his beautiful wife Shana and now has two gorgeous children, Harry and Poppy.

Tony gained a 2:1 Honours degree in Business and Marketing from Manchester University before travelling the world for a year.

Tony has over 15 years' experience in sales, both business to business and business to consumer, and has trained over 3,000 sales professionals in a variety of industries. Tony started his career as a telesales consultant for the largest outsourced call centre, where he was involved in selling business to consumer for one of the UK's biggest utility providers. He was awarded salesperson of the month for six consecutive months and was then moved into a training role where he wrote scripts and rebuttals and trained every new consultant before they went on the phone.

Tony then moved into a business to business environment selling address management solutions. He started by cold calling and generating appointments at director level and then sold in the field. He then progressed within a year, training a team of fourteen telesales executives how to make appointments from cold calling and focusing his time on blue-chip clients. In his four years at the company, he sold the highest value order of £725,000 over a three year contract.

Alongside his business partner, Boyd Mayover, Tony's father-in-law, they set up a sales training company in May 2006. He started by cold calling to generate appointments for both himself and his partner Boyd. Within the first year, they had 56 clients and this has continued to grow year on year. In six and a half years, it has accumulated to over 280 clients across 75 different industries. The company recently rebranded and is now called the Sales Doctor.

Tony's ethos is you can sell any product or service with the right attitude and a well planned call structure.

Tony grew up in Borehamwood, Hertfordshire and now lives in Shenley, Hertfordshire. He enjoys spending time with his family, watching films, reading and shopping.

www.wedosalestraining.com

"I've failed over and over and over again in my life and that is why I succeed."

Michael Jordan

"Pretend that every single person you meet has a sign around his or her neck that says, 'Make me feel important.' Not only will you succeed in sales, you will succeed in life."

Mary Kay Ash

Why did I write this book?

My career has always been in sales. I started at the age of 15, working in retail at weekends. To pay for university, I had a few sales jobs from selling newspaper subscriptions door to door, doing telesales selling double glazing and selling mobile phones in a call centre. After graduating, I sold encyclopaedias door to door in Australia to fund the final few months of my travels.

On return from travelling, I sold utilities over the phone for the largest outsourced call centre and was awarded top salesperson for six consecutive months out of 65 people. I was then promoted to train all the telesales executives and write the scripts and rebuttals (objection handlers). I moved into a business to business position to sell IT software.

I began as a telesales executive and my role was to make appointments over the phone for the field sales reps. I was the fastest salesperson to progress to a field sales rep within eight months and was given the additional role of training the telesales team. I was the first sales consultant to generate over £3m worth of new business and was allocated five blue-chip clients to manage.

After progressing as high as I could, I set up a sales training company called Positive Approach in May 2006 with my business partner. I generated new business by cold calling, and within the first year, had brought on 57 clients from a standing start. I took on an additional 40 clients in the second year and then recruited a telesales team.

In May 2011, we rebranded the business to The Sales Doctor and to date we have over 300 clients across 70 industries. I have personally delivered training to over 3,000 sales professionals from people with all different levels of experience and across all verticals.

I believe I am the best suited person to write this book as I have been very successful in sales and am able to clearly explain the reasons behind my success. I have always been good at telling stories and explaining things to people and make things easy to understand. With both my varied sales and training experiences, I have great all round knowledge to share with readers.

I am living proof that my sales techniques work and am still learning every single day. I have had many failings along the way; however, I have learnt invaluable lessons from these which I am able to share with others and provide my readers with a different perspective on success and failure.

"Success depends
upon previous preparation,
and without such preparation
there is sure to be failure."

Confucius

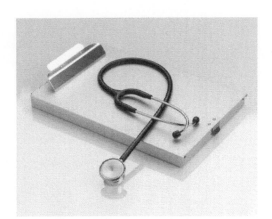

Dear Sales Doctor...

The top 66 answers to real sales challenges

Tony Morris

Published by
Filament Publishing Ltd
16, Croydon Road, Waddon, Croydon,
Surrey, CRO 4PA, United Kingdom
Telephone +44 (0)20 8688 2598
Fax +44 (0)20 7183 7186
info@filamentpublishing.com
www.filamentpublishing.com

ISBN 978-1-910125-06-9
Printed by Berforts Information Press
Stevenage & Hastings

Dedication

Growing up, I never had an uncle or a great uncle and meeting my wife's great uncle filled that void for me. Ken was one of the kindest and most helpful individuals I have ever had the fortune to spend time with. Although he wasn't a blood relation, he treated me like one, and we spent days discussing his success and experiences as an insurance salesman and he taught me so much that I can use in my own career, which I am forever grateful.

He dedicated so much time to help me with my first book, 'Coffee's for Closers' and he kindly offered to help with this book, until he unfortunately became too ill. I miss him dearly and hope I can be half the sales professional that he once was!

"Sales are contingent upon the attitude of the salesman - not the attitude of the prospect."

W. Clement Stone

Contents

Tip 1

Dear Sales Doctor,

I am struggling to get the best out of my sales team. What do you suggest to keep them constantly motivated?

There are many debates about which the most effective style of management is and which achieves the best results. We have all heard the 'carrot and the stick' analogy time and time again. It's fair to say that one style of management does not fit all and it's all about learning how to adapt to the individual member of your team to gain the best possible results.

One of the best lessons I learnt in management is what motivates me, does not necessarily motivate my team. My job as a successful manager is to understand what motivates the individuals within my team and remind them of those key drivers every day.

Many salespeople are financially motivated and they say, "I simply want to earn lots of money." In my experience, the more specific the better, it becomes much more motivational. You would hardly go into the gym and say I'd like to become a beef cake.

I remember in 2005 when I decided it was time to propose. My first task was to enquire about an engagement ring and so off with the mother-in-law I went. At £2,000, I thought this was going to take me forever, as I was only able to put away around £20 a month. So I set myself goals and broke it down specifically. At the time, I was selling software and had a very transparent commission structure.

So I gave myself six months to save for a ring, so I needed to save £333 a month to achieve my goal. This was £83.25 per week and I worked out an average order value for commission was £45 per deal, so I required two extra deals a week to hit my goal. My conversion rate at that time was 1 in 2.5 meetings turned into business, so I needed to attend a further five meetings per week. As I monitored and measured my figures very closely, I was aware that I needed to make 68 calls to get hold of five decision makers a day and I converted 1 in 2 to a meeting. So I needed to make an additional 28 calls a day, to get hold of an additional two decision makers, which would enable me to get that extra one meeting. By being this specific every day, I knew clearly what was required and I wouldn't leave the office until I had made my desired call rate. I am pleased to say I achieved this goal in four months and she said "YES".

I always recommend managers tell their sales team to establish what you are looking to achieve and break it into digestible chunks, no matter how big the goal seems. If your goals are tangible, such as a new car, I have seen many of my clients have a print-out of their exact car, colour and model they desire placed in front of them on their desk. Their visual reminder every day keeps up their motivation and is a daily reminder of why they are working. So when it gets to 17:28 and normally they'll be thinking about what they are having for dinner or who are they meeting in the pub, their mind can remain focused on their goal. It can drive them to make those extra calls that are needed to achieve their end result.

As a sales and management trainer, I have been fortunate to work with over a thousand managers in a variety of different businesses and industries. I have seen some incredible managers who inspire their team on a daily basis to continually strive to outperform themselves and I have seen the 'David Brent' type of manager, without the humour.

One thing I see far too often is the manager continually pointing out to their sales team things that they are doing wrong; even though they label it as constructive feedback, as opposed to criticism, it still can lead to a demotivated and frustrated sales team. What I always recommend to sales managers is 'catch them doing something right'.

Even if it's the smallest thing, it always has a more positive and beneficial effect on the individual. One example of this is if you hear your sales person make a sales call that you feel was awful, try and highlight one positive from the call i.e. you asked great questions on that call or that was a great opening gambit. If the same mistakes keeps happening with the individual, then it must be delivered in a positive manner, such as "I heard that call, by the way, and your opening was excellent, a great benefit statement. I would recommend asking a few more open questions as you will definitely get the prospect sharing more information and it demonstrates that you are interested in them. Keep up the good work as you make more calls than everyone in the team, which is admirable."

"Learn from the past,
set vivid,
detailed goals
for the future,
and live in the
only moment of time
over which you
have any control:
now."

Denis Waitley

"I used to say 'Things cost too much.'
Then my teacher straightened
me out on that by saying,
'The problem isn't that things
cost too much.
The problem is that
you can't afford it.'
That's when I finally understood
that the problem wasn't 'it' -
the problem was 'me'."

Jim Rohn

Tip 2

Dear Sales Doctor,

More often than not, my prospective customer says my product is 'too expensive' and I find this really difficult to overcome, as we are more expensive than our competitors. My boss won't allow us to drop our prices so I'm losing loads of deals as a result. Any ideas?

This is extremely common in sales and it's all about adding value as opposed to dropping your price. Think about it; when the prospect says 'too expensive', what does that actually mean? To me, there are four meanings available; firstly, they can't afford it, secondly, they don't see the value, thirdly, they have seen it cheaper elsewhere, or finally, they are negotiating.

Therefore, my first question to your prospective customer when they say you are "too expensive" would be, "What are you comparing us against?"

For argument's sake let's imagine your product is £1,000 and your competitor is £700, so your prospective customer is comparing you to that competitor. You need to find out what the prospective customer gets for £700; get them to list out everything that's included in that price. Your job now is to sell all the additional benefits you bring to the table FOR ONLY £300! SELL THE DIFFERENCE. You are no longer talking about £1,000; you are simply selling yourselves for £300.

It's very rare that both yours and your competitor's offerings are identical, so you should be able to find at least three examples of additional benefits that you can offer over and above your competition. I can give you one for starters; YOU. I always say to my prospective customers, "There is no Tony Morris being offered and I will be your dedicated consultant, at your beck and call whenever you need me".

"So much of life
is a negotiation -
so even if you're
not in business,
you have opportunities
to practice all around you."

Kevin O'Leary

Tip 3

Dear Sales Doctor,

I manage a sales team and am no longer at the sharp end; my team keep telling me sales has changed dramatically in the past decade. Do you agree with this?

In this current economic climate, buyers being more cautious with spending their budgets than ever before, and now is the pivotal time a sales professional must always be on his 'A Game'.

It's all about being able to demonstrate how you can add value to your customers and be a source of both knowledge and expertise in your field. Two decades ago, selling was all about selling a product or service to your customers; I believe things have taken a full 360 degrees and now it's all about 'helping people buy'. In order to help your customers buy, you must understand exactly what they want and their reasoning behind this desire, and then recommend a solution. Notice I used the word 'recommend'; after all, what are we if we are not recommenders or trusted advisors?

Let me illustrate this. You walk into a doctor's surgery and see Doctor Number 1 and say, "Doctor I hope you can help, I have a splitting headache." He replies, "Take some paracetamol and if the pain persists, please come back to and see me."

I then walk in and see Doctor Number 2 and say, "I hope you can help, I have a splitting headache." The doctor offers me a seat.

Dr: Where in your head is the pain?

Me: In my temples.

Dr: When in the day do get these headaches?

Me: Normally the morning.

Dr: How long have you been suffering?

Me: About a month in total.

Dr: How much liquid do you drink in the day?

Me: About a litre, I guess

Dr: On a scale of 1 to 10, 10 being excruciating pain, where would you describe your pain?

Me: I suppose a 7 at its worst.

Dr: From what you've described, I would recommend paracetamol. If the pain persists, come back and see me.

Which doctor would you rather see? I would assume the latter would be your answer.

Which doctor is better medically trained? We don't really know, they could be as qualified as each other.

So why did you choose Doctor 2? What did he demonstrate that the first doctor didn't?

He showed his credibility, clearly took an interest in me, gave me absolute confidence that he knew what he was doing. So by asking a few open questions, my perception was, he was far more professional and a much better doctor.

Tip 4

Dear Sales Doctor,

I sell out in the field and it can be quite a lonely job sometimes. There are weeks where I am out doing appointments and door knocking and although I haven't achieved any sales, I had an okay week. I walk into my office on a Friday and my boss asks me immediately, "How many deals have you done this week?" to which I reply, "None". "What kind of salesman are you if you can't close a deal? And what have you been doing, watching Countdown? Why are you back in the office if you haven't done any business? Go out there and close."

How the hell do I stay motivated and positive when I get that response every time I walk into the office without a sale?

This is very common for remote field salespeople, so let me ask you some questions.

"What did you achieve that week?" He replied, "Weren't you listening, I got no sales at all, so nothing," he angrily rebutted. I argued the point and said, "I guarantee you did achieve things, you are just closed off to it right now."

Me: How many new opportunities did you find that week that you didn't have at the beginning of the week?

Salesman: Well, about eight I guess, but surely if I didn't close them, it's irrelevant?

Me: And out of those eight, how many decision makers' names did you identify?

Salesman: All of them, what's your point?

Me: Did you find out the situation within those eight companies?

Salesman: Yeah, I found out the supplier they are with, the products they use and their contract date, but I didn't close any of them.

Me: What you are missing is you are in a better position now than you were at the beginning of the week, as you have identified eight new businesses with which you will be able to work. If you stay in touch with them, there's a very strong possibility one of their suppliers will mess up and you can get in immediately.

Equally, I would rather 10% of something than 100% of nothing, so it's worth positioning yourself as their back-up supplier. You clearly qualified the prospect, so who's to say in the near future their requirements don't change and they may need something you offer that their suppliers cannot.

So the key is **focus on what you did get, as opposed to focusing on what you didn't**. There will be days where you get hold of 40 companies that, for whatever reason, you cannot help. Rather than hang yourself, understand that you had to call those 40 at some point, so at least you got them out of the way.

Tip 5

Dear Sales Doctor,

I currently outsource all inbound calls to an external company. Do you think it's okay to do that or would you suggest recruiting a receptionist?

As we are coming out of one of the worst recessions our economy has ever experienced, it's more important now than ever to provide exceptional customer service on every call. Many businesses say "Cash is king"; I strongly disagree and say "Customer is king" and cash comes second.

It has been proven time and time again that if you do a good job, someone will tell one person, and if you do a bad job, someone will tell 10 people. Think of the last time you had a great meal in a restaurant and an awful meal; which one did you tell people most about? With the social media book, this is magnified a thousand times.

The customer must experience a consistent level of exceptional service from anyone they deal with. 86% of customers quit doing business with a company because of a bad customer experience, up from 59% four years ago (*Source: Harris Interactive, Customer Experience Impact Report*). Therefore, bad service can kill a company and everyone in your organisation must be on board and aligned.

It often astonishes me how poorly many receptionists or salespeople answer the phone. When are companies going to realise that the first point of contact is the ONLY one that matters? If the first point of contact is poor, why should I ever listen or call back?

How familiar are these statements to you; "Name, postcode, who wants him? What's it about?" These were all designed by a sales prevention officer. It all seems easy, doesn't it? We answer the phone in a professional corporate manner and show that we care for each individual customer.

They could be a customer today or maybe in three months; time. They could be making a complaint that we believe is unreasonable. SO WHAT!! The idea that we would have a great business if our customers understood us is becoming far too prevalent in the UK today and will kill business at a time when everyone should be looking to do more, manage customers' expectations, and ensure their experience with our company is a great one.

A client of mine was having a problem with retaining customers, and when we looked into the situation properly, we found out that because he was very busy, the incoming calls were too high for his receptionist to handle and therefore, rather than tell him, she just rushed people off the phone. 50% of new callers don't ring back if they don't get an answer when they call, and 15% of existing customers don't call again if they get the same experience! (*Source: Moneypenny*)

This was handled easily by doing two things. 1. Retraining the receptionist. 2. Using the phone system to better effect so that calls were diverted to the right people. This is not always that easy to handle. We must be aware of the short and long-term damage a poor initial response will give.

Do you know how your phones are being answered? Do you check? If we want to be the best of the best, we must start looking at all areas of our business. We cannot say, "Oh, she's just the receptionist" or "My people are very busy." Spend time and money now on training and extolling your ethos and reap the rewards. The alternative is too horrific to think about; these statistics are just an indication of this:

73% of consumers end a relationship due to poor service and the root causes are:

- Having to repeat information
- Feeling trapped in automated self-service
- Having to wait too long
- Interacting with staff who have no knowledge of the service history (or customer value)
- Unable to easily switch between communication channels

(Source: Genesys Telecommunications Laboratories Report – The Cost of Poor Customer Service)

On the flip side of the coin, in a business to business engagement, delighted customers are five times more likely to plan on repurchasing than merely satisfied customers. (*Source: Ipsos Loyalty Report: The role of customer delight in achieving customer loyalty*)

"The golden rule for every business man is this: 'Put yourself in your customer's place.'"

Orison Swett Marden

"Everyone lives by selling something."

Robert Louis Stevenson

Tip 6

Dear Sales Doctor,

I'm in two minds whether cold calling works anymore. What's your opinion on it?

I don't believe cold calling does work anymore, though I know smart calling works. Smart calling is being a little bit smart before the call and doing a little bit of homework. I would recommend no more than three minutes as you may end up with a voicemail. Cold calling is where you literally are going in cold, no contact name, no idea about the company or industry you are calling, no angle as to how to you can help or add value to the business etc. Many sales gurus claim cold calling doesn't work anymore as buyers have wised up to them, and to some extent I agree. However, smart calling does work. I have learned some wonderful ideas and techniques from a fantastic US sales guru Art Sobczak.

When preparing to make a smart call, there are certain steps I always think about.

Step 1: What does the company actually do that I am about to call? Once I know this, I can think of any companies similar to them I may have helped and be prepared to name-drop them, if appropriate. I can prepare a couple of facts of how I have been able to help those companies as well i.e. increase their conversion rates by 30%, reduce their lead costs by 25% etc.

Step 2: Who do I actually want to speak to within the business? Who is likely to be the decision maker? I can look on the website and there is normally a 'Meet the Team' page or an 'About Us' page and within that content, there should be a name.

Now this may not be the contact you require. However, once you have a name, you can use it. You can say to the gatekeeper, "I have been recommended to speak to John Doe but I don't believe he is the right person. Who would you suggest I speak to regarding.........?" The gatekeeper will be slightly more receptive than if you just said, "Who can I speak to regarding my products and services?"

OPENING STATEMENTS HAVE A WIIFM (What's in it for me)

Step 3: Prepare your opening statement; this is the reason why a prospect should take your call. When you make a call, don't tell people what you do; tell people what you have done, successfully, with companies like theirs. Let me give you an example for my sales training business when calling an estate agent.

Example A:

"Good morning Mr Estate Agent, thanks for taking my call. My name is Tony Morris and I am the director of the Sales Doctor. We deliver bespoke training and cover an array of courses from sales through to management. The reason for my call today is to see how are you developing your negotiators?"

Example B:

"Good morning Mr Estate Agent, thanks for taking my call. My name is Tony Morris and I am the director of the Sales Doctor. Are you familiar with my business?"

"Yes" – "Great, as you are probably aware...

OR

"No" – "Okay, to make you aware.....

"We have been successfully delivering training to many estate agents like A, B and C (name-drop ones they'd have heard of) by helping negotiators qualify applicants more effectively, resulting in more qualified viewings and a significant increase in deals being tied.

"In this market, our clients have found one of the biggest challenges they face is lack of stock. How have you found this at the moment?" [Very likely to be the same, if it's a big problem for the majority.]

"To help our clients, we have provided the negotiators with some innovative techniques to gain more private landlord details and then trained them to cold call the landlords, which have resulted in an increase in valuations being made.

"So the reason for my call today is to see if we can help your team too. So how are you currently developing your negotiators?"

I hope you'll agree example B is better than the previous example, and all I did differently was explain very briefly how I have helped businesses like theirs. Now there may be situations where you haven't helped companies in their industry; so for this you need to think of examples where you have helped companies that have faced similar challenges to them.

This happened very recently in my business. We were approached by a very big publishing company to train their 40 inbound salespeople. I knew we hadn't worked with companies in the publishing industry so I found out what challenges their salespeople faced and the key areas they felt needed developing. Fortunately, I had trained a big tour operator who had a large inbound sales team who had similar issues and challenges, and I explained very clearly what I covered with them and, most importantly, the benefits they received as a result of it.

"If eighty percent
of your sales
come from
twenty percent of
all of your items,
just carry those
twenty percent."

Henry A. Kissinger

Tip 7

Dear Sales Doctor,

Have you got any tips for making a follow-up call?

Let's imagine that you've placed a great first call to a prospect... Qualified them, generated interest, identified a need, sent the literature, and now it's time to call back and close the sale. It should be easy, and require little selling, right? WRONG!

Here's one very important point regarding follow-up calls, and everything else will revolve around this point: You need to do as much, or more, selling on the follow-up call as you did on the initial call.

A mistake that even the best telephone sales reps make is that they assume the prospect will be ready to buy on the second call, because the first call went so well. As a result, calls with opening statements similar to these are:

CALLER 1: "Hi Steve, this is Bill Scott at Allen Industries. Do you have any questions on the information I sent you?"

CALLER 2: "Kathy, this is Mark Smith calling back from Gateway Supply. Did you get the literature I sent?"

CALLER 3: "Mr. Webber, I'm Sue Chambers with Anthony Equipment. I sent you our proposal, and was wondering what you thought about it."

Those opening statements are horrible, since none state what is in it for the prospect, and they marginally explain the reason for the call.

Needs to Be As Strong As Initial Call

Your opening statement on the follow-up call needs to be as strong as your opener on the initial call you placed. The reasoning is that although **you** may have a vivid recollection of what you discussed on the first call, *they* might not even **remember** you right away. They probably have spoken with 30 or 40 other salespeople since then. Therefore, on your follow-up call opening statement, you need to add one more component to the three questions you must answer for the prospect, and that is to remind them that you spoke before. Even if you have a phone appointment, and they are expecting your call, remind them of what you discussed so that you can quickly move into the call. For example:

CALLER: "Hello Mr. Whittaker, this is Tony Morris with Sales Doctor. The reason for the call is to continue our conversation of last Monday, when we were discussing how you could increase your sales conversions by 10% with no increase in costs. I'd like to go over three of the points I highlighted in the literature you were sent... Is that package handy?"

With this opening, the caller identified herself, gave the reason for the call, which was to continue the conversation, reminded the prospect of what they spoke about the first time and mentioned a benefit, and referred to the literature, and asked if it were handy.

Assume They Received Literature

Notice that the caller didn't say, "Did you get it?" You should assume that they did receive your material. Beginning a call with the poor examples we mentioned earlier is awkward, and leaves the caller nowhere to go.

As mentioned earlier, the most important point to remember about follow-up calls is that you need to continue selling. After all, if they were ready to buy, they would have called you, right? Too many salespeople make the mistake of calling back, and hope that the prospect is going to say, "OK, it looks good, I'm ready to buy." That rarely is the case.

Tip 8

Dear Sales Doctor,

Is sales a numbers game?

In my opinion, sales is only a numbers game if done correctly! I am one of the worst footballers you could ever meet and if I took 100 penalties against an average keeper, I may score three by pure luck alone. If you took a footballer that had some ability, who practised on a regular basis, developed their penalty taking skills and then shot 100 penalties against an average keeper, do you think they might score more than three goals? So it's a smart numbers game, meaning the better you are, and the more you do, the better results you will achieve; however, you need both to achieve great success.

An extract from Chapter 1 of my book, 'Coffee's for Closers': When I'm cold calling on the phone and crunching those numbers, I apply a similar approach and mind set to the smart numbers game as above. I often think back to a time when I was travelling in Sydney, Australia. I was eight months into my travels and had almost run out of money and had to get my head round the frightening reality of having to return home and enter back into normal life and find a job. I was chatting to an Aussie guy on Bondi Beach who looked the spitting image of Mick Jagger in his younger years. I was moaning about my financial situation when he said, "I have been running a direct sales operation for the past six years selling encyclopaedias and I have 130 sales reps selling door to door. Why don't you come and work for me?" he said. Intrigued, I asked him, "How does it work?" and he took me back to his house, which I can only describe as the most beautiful castle I had ever laid eyes on. In his office, he showed me a giant map of Sydney and the surrounding areas all highlighted in different colours, which marked the different sales reps' territories.

He showed me what would be my territory and handed me this 2,800 page book and a rucksack and said, "You need to go door knocking and have to close on the day. Every encyclopaedia you sell, you will earn $150 cash in hand." I was out the door before he said "hand" and on I went.

I started the following morning and left my hostel at 08:30 to walk to my first road in 79 degrees heat. I was so keen and had already spent my newly earned commission in my head. I arrived at the start of my first road and excitedly knocked on my first door. After eight knocks, I realised this was what they describe in sales as time wasting. I knocked on my second, then my third, my fourth and by my fifth, no answer. I started to think were these houses actually inhabited! It wasn't until my 8th door where a cute older lady aged around 110 answered the door and she had to go and fetch her hearing aid to hear my pitch – "Great start", I thought to myself, "the first person I actually get to pitch is deaf". After 25 minutes of screaming at her and watching patiently as she fiddled with her hearing aid, I made the executive decision I was barking up the wrong tree and on I went.

I kept on knocking, and on my 34th door, a young guy opened the door and I thought, "This is my opportunity". As soon as I uttered the words "Hi, my name is Tony", BANG and I am now pitching to a door! I started having second thoughts and looked at my watch to realise I'd been walking a total of 33 minutes and I was already considering quitting. I remembered my Dad's words, "in sales you never quit" and on I went. I must have knocked on about 75 doors and spoken to one person who allowed me to get my pitch out to which he replied quite politely, "Never come here again." When I realised he was the nicest person I'd spoken to all day, I realised I chose the wrong area and back to the hostel it was.

The following day, my alarm went off at 07:55am and I jumped in the shower and got out on the road, full of the same level of enthusiasm as yesterday morning, as I chanted to myself 'new day, new opportunities.' By 16:45 and now the 12 people I spoke to had all told me where to go, my chant home was very different. When I woke up the following day, I thought I'm going to give it my final go as maybe sales just isn't for me.

I went on my way and got an answer at my first door, and the lady actually let me get my two minute pitch out to which she replied, "How much?" in a shocked intake of breath. I explained the encyclopaedias normally retailed at $499; however, we are running an amazing promotion and selling them for ONLY $399 (word for word what my script said) and she invited me in. I almost high-fived her but thought that may show a sign of desperation so high-fived myself in my head. She kindly made me a cold drink and started to look through this huge book that I had been carrying round on my back for the past 48 hours which was starting to create an imprint on my skin. It wasn't until her husband came down the stairs to join us, and within a matter of seconds kindly asked me to leave, and I left to him shouting at her to not invite strangers in. The rest of my day was pretty much déjà vu and by 3pm when the final door was slammed in my face, I thought going back to the UK was more appealing than this and I accepted defeat graciously!

I went straight back to Mr Jagger's castle to return this stupid unsellable big book. With sweat on my brow and big sweat rings under my arms, he looked at me like some vagrant and said, "You look a mess, let me get you a drink". My second invitation in three days although I was pretty confident he wouldn't listen to my pitch either. I said, "It's impossible; I simply don't believe anyone sells these things." He laughed and said, "I have one question for you, how many doors did you knock on a day?" Surprised by his question, I shrugged my shoulders and said, "I didn't really count but I guess around 70 a day." He replied, "I chose not to share this with you as I wanted you to learn for yourself, however all my reps. measure their figures. They have proven that you must knock on a minimum of 100 doors per day. Only nine people will listen to you pitch and six of them will tell you where to go, some politely and some not, three, however, will invite you in. Two of these will politely SELL TO YOU a reason why they can't buy today such as 'I need to think about it', 'I don't have the money',' I'm not sure I'll use it' etc. However, one will buy – GUARANTEED". The numbers never lie." To say I was sceptical was an understatement and I remember saying, "I knocked on at least 200 doors throughout the three days". He interrupted me and reiterated 100 per day minimum.

He said, "You have two days left of this week and surely it's worth trying, or maybe sales is not your bag and you should get a cleaner's job," and with that I grabbed my book back and went on my way.

14 no answer, 15 no answer, 16 no...... And the door opened. "Hi, my name is Tony Morris and I have an incredible promotion available for today only...". and he listened to my pitch and then slammed the door in my face. Before screaming obscenities through his letter box, I took a deep breath and thought about what Mr Jagger had said, "Nine will listen and six will tell you where to go," so I had eight to go according to him. I kept on knocking and number 31 invited me in. She sat me down and listened intently and then dropped the bombshell: "I need to think about it," and on the outside I was smiling, although I am pretty sure she could see me grinding my teeth in anger. However, keeping the tally, I continued my walk. Lucky number 67 was what I named Mr Peterson and to this day, I remember that feeling as he pulled out his cheque book. I called Mr Jagger to organise an encyclopaedia to be delivered to the door and, restraining myself from screaming down the phone, I calmly switched my mobile off and continued grinning. As he shook my hand, I went in for the man hug, to which he stood there still as a mannequin as I hugged him, until I felt I was invading his personal space. I skipped out of his house and did one of those jumps where you click your heels together and almost tripped over his front garden. I carried on knocking as I was convinced I was on a lucky streak. 33 rejections later, I went back to the hostel with the biggest smile on my face and a feeling I will never forget. No word of a lie, I continued this job for the next six weeks and my feelings towards having the door slammed in my face took a full 360 degrees. When door no. 24 was slammed hard in my face, I clenched a fist of delight and muttered to myself, "Another 66 to go until I get somewhere".

Mr Jagger was right, the figures never lied. People thought I was actually insane when they shouted at me, "I never want to see your face again" and I replied with a big grin plastered across my face, "Good you are the 59t hperson to say that to me today, so I need 31 more of them." This was one of my first, yet most vital lessons in sales. It's a numbers game as long as you learn your pitch well and give it the same level of enthusiasm and passion every opportunity you obtain you cannot fail.

Tip 9

Dear Sales Doctor,

Should you leave voicemails when cold calling?

That's a great question and I would definitely recommend you leave a voicemail, as long as it's the right message. Many salespeople I train leave the following type of voicemail:

"Good afternoon, Mr Morris, this is John Smith calling from ABC systems. I am calling to see if you'd be interested in our new IT software that is used for creating your own email campaigns. If so, please call me back on 0800 121212."

Now, the chances of getting a reply to that is one in a million and is based 100% on pure luck. You may have called the right person at the right time who is looking for the type of product or service you are offering and will return your call. However, we know in sales you never rely on luck, you create your own luck!

When leaving a voicemail, like any cold call, you need to think about your objective of the call. Quite simply it's to get the prospect to return your call. So I suggest the following two messages:

The first I call the ambiguous voicemail, as you do not mention the reason for the call, your company name, and you use informal language to give the impression the prospect should know who you are, creating curiosity. Here is an example:

"Hi John, Tony here. Give me a bell when you get this on 020 7212 3344. Cheers."

I always leave this type of message to directors of companies and get approx. 60% return rate. When they call me back and ask what's it regarding, I thank them for returning my call and go into my well prepared opening benefit statement discussing how I have helped companies like theirs and want to discuss how I may be able to help them also.

The second type of voicemail I call the urgency voicemail. This is where you need to sound serious and ask to be called back immediately. However, it's important to note you must have an angle for this call when you get a call back. For example, if you sell advertising space, you could say you had a last minute cancellation and have one space available at a hugely discounted rate. The voicemail sounds like this:

"Hi John, It's Tony here. Can you call me back as a matter of urgency on 020 7212 2344. Thanks."

Now go and try these and let me know how you get on.

"You cannot control what happens to you, but you can control your attitude toward what happens to you, and in that, you will be mastering change rather than allowing it to master you."

Brian Tracy

Tip 10

Dear Sales Doctor,

I get many web enquiries from influencers or PAs who have to report back to the ultimate decision maker. How do I handle that without being rude and asking to speak to their boss?

This is a question I get very often in my sales training courses and it is challenging. You are right that you don't want to offend them by either asking to speak their boss or by going above their head anyway and contacting the boss. This is what I always recommend:

Once you have truly qualified the enquiry and found as much information as you possibly can, ask them the following question: "Aside from yourself, John, who else needs to get involved in making the decision?" Now, more often or not, they'll simply respond by saying, "My boss or the managing director." Reply by saying, "For my records, what's the name of your boss?"

Now you have the decision maker's name, I would ask them, "What will Bob base his decision on?" or "What are Bob's three key priorities when choosing a XXX supplier?" Write down their words very carefully taking special note of the exact language they use to describe things. The reason for this is you can use those exact words back to them in your proposal or any future correspondence with them, which will give them the impression that you think the same as them. Remember, if we see the world through John Smith's eyes, we are more likely to get John Smith to buy from us.

Depending on what product/ service you sell and the value of your offering, I always recommend arranging a meeting with the prospective customer.

I would position it by saying, "I really would like to meet you, John, as I value your thoughts and opinions. Do you want to invite Bob along or should I speak to him?" This very assumptive question keeps the influencer or PA in the loop and embeds the seed that Bob the MD needs to be involved. Very often, John will reply, "I don't need to be involved. However, I'll get dates that Bob is available and get back to you". This is the answer you wanted in the first place.

If John responds, "I just want your literature at this point, as I am speaking to a few suppliers and Bob just wants to look at this before agreeing to meet anybody," I would suggest saying the following, "I understand that. However, my literature will not be able to answer both yours and Bob's questions as it's generic. Equally, John, you are an expert at what you do and I am an expert at what I do; the last thing I want to happen is Bob ask you some questions about my offering and you are unable to answer them.

"Alternatively, you may provide him with the wrong information which would affect the decision he makes. I would strongly recommend I come in and meet Bob to answer any questions he may have as a result of reading my generic literature and therefore providing him with everything he needs to make an informed decision. I am available to meet Bob next Tuesday or Thursday, what date is best for him?"

Tip 11

Dear Sales Doctor,

I have recently joined an email marketing company as a new business sales executive and I have been receiving very bad feedback about how my company has dealt with people in the past. I really don't know how to overcome this. Any suggestions?

As you are a new member of staff and haven't been privy to what's gone on previously in the company, it's very difficult to comment on what's happened. Your objective is to reassure the prospective customer that things have changed and educate them on how you can now help them in moving forward. This can only be achieved by understanding exactly what occurred in the past and then using the third party proof technique (FEEL, FELT, FOUND) to put their mind at rest. Let me demonstrate in the following example.

Prospect customer: I appreciate the call. However, I had such a bad experience in the past with your company that I do not wish to take this conversation any further.

Sales executive: I really am sorry to hear that. May I ask what actually happened?

Prospect customer: The sales guy I dealt with promised me many things with the email campaigns I purchased and failed to deliver on them. So naturally, I have lost complete faith in your business all together.

Sales executive: I don't blame you for that. If I was in your shoes, I would feel exactly the same way. Just to clarify, what was it you were promised that you didn't receive?

Prospect customer: The sales guy ensured me I would receive regular updates on the campaign activity and from memory I received two reports over three months, which were not particularly clear, to say the least.

Sales executive: That really is disgraceful and I can only apologise that you experienced that with our business. You mentioned regular updates; in an ideal world, how often would you like to be updated and what would be important for you to see on a report?

Prospect customer: I asked to see things such as the number of emails opened, bounce rates, undeliverable email address etc. As long as the report is clear and simple to read, I am happy.

Sales executive: I have taken on board all your feedback and I sincerely appreciate you taking the time to share it with me. I really do understand how you **FEEL**. I have had a couple clients who have **FELT** exactly the same. However, what they have now **FOUND** with our business is all email campaign reporting is online and can be viewed on a daily basis if the client wishes. We can tailor the report around your requirements, to show as much, or as little, information as you would like to see. As the new sales executive in your area, I want to demonstrate how we have grown and developed as a business and gain your valued feedback. I am available on Wednesday and Friday next week; which day is most convenient for yourself?

I hope this example demonstrates that what started off as an understandably defensive prospect, that by asking a lot of probing questions and using the third party proof, you are able to turn a prospect around and build their confidence back up.

Tip 12

Dear Sales Doctor,

I have been doing sales for about six months and every time I think I'm getting better, I get rejected and knocked back down again and don't think I can handle picking myself up again and again. Any suggestions?

One inevitable part of sales that can never be avoided is - rejection. However, it's only rejection if you label it rejection. Many people say the person is not rejecting YOU, they are rejecting the idea, product or service that you are proposing. I completely disagree with this concept and they are 100% rejecting YOU. So you need to review the call and think, did I sound boring? Did I sound disinterested? Did I have a good enough opening gambit that engaged the prospect and created some desire? Think about it, if the person wasn't rejecting you, then why do some people take a sales call and some don't? Is it purely on the product or service that's being offered? Of course not!

It's imperative that you do not take it personally; otherwise sales is not right for you. If you get upset every time someone puts the phone down on you or is rude to you, then you are definitely in the wrong profession. You require rhino skin, yet equally you don't keep calling and getting rejected until one person is receptive to you. You review, tweak and dust yourself off and try again. Remember, perfect practice makes perfect. Not what most people believe, practice makes perfect. If you saw me hit 100 golf balls badly in the range and then saw me mess up on a golf course, you'll understand that if I kept on practising my awful swing I would not get anywhere fast. However, if I was shown by a professional how to swing properly, then it's worth practising that. Make sense?

It's only rejection if you label it rejection. So if my objective of the call is to make an appointment and I walk away with the decision maker's name and number, then that's a result. Alternatively, I may make 50 calls, all of which I may decide they have no requirement for what I'm selling. Now rather than walk away feeling rejected, I view it as I had to make those 50 calls at some point, and at least I have got them out the way and can move on.

'Failures not the falling down, but it's the staying down'

As I mentioned earlier, there is no such thing as rejection, it's feedback. Change 'I failed' to 'I've learned what never to do again'. Many salespeople view 'no' as one step closer to a 'yes'. When you get rejected, go back to the prospect and say, "I appreciate we are not doing business at this juncture, however, so that I can learn from this, and my company can improve and develop, what could I have done differently to be successful?" The day is not bad unless you name it bad. Rather than invest your time and energy moaning about something, use your creativity to think up a solution.

"A rejection is nothing more than a necessary step in the pursuit of success."

Bo Bennett

Tip 13

Dear Sales Doctor,

I often find myself pitching to the wrong person who claims to be the decision maker and it turns out another person needs to be involved in the decision making process. Is there anything I can do to avoid this?

It's always a difficult one because if you ask the prospect if they are the decision maker and they say they are, you can't start accusing them of lying! There are some set questions I always recommend to ask, which reduces your chances of this happening; however, I wish I'd have taken my own advice with a big hotel group I train.

I cold called this particular hotel group and asked the receptionist, "Who is responsible for choosing external training companies to work with?" and she replied, "The head of learning and development and her name is Jane Smith".

For many weeks, after leaving voicemail after voicemail, email after email (I even managed to get Jane's mobile number and left numerous message and texts), she finally came back to me after three months of persistent calling to ask, "What's it regarding?" I explained I deliver sales training to many hotel groups and started to explain how I have helped them, when Jane stopped me in my tracks and explained her remit is to select companies to deliver health & safety training, legal training, IT skills etc. and sales training has nothing to do with her.

I began to think back to that annoying receptionist and started to curse her in my mind. However, on reflection, had she done anything wrong?

Not at all, she was right in saying that Jane was responsible for choosing external training companies, just not sales training companies, which

I foolishly didn't ask. Jane kindly gave me the right contact and within a month, they were a client of mine, just three months later than they should have been.

When I am in front of a prospective customer, I now ask the following: "Aside from yourself, John, who else needs to be involved in making the decision?" By asking this question in such a way, it avoids any offence and allows the prospect to share any other people who are involved in the decision making process.

If they say they are the sole decision maker, I ask as well as making the decision, "Do you sign off the budgets?" If other contact names are mentioned I ask, "What will you base the ultimate decision on and what are important to both you and X?" This gets the prospect to share his, and his peer's, priorities.

After my lesson learned with my hotel client, when I am given a contact name, I always ask who they report to. If they are the top of the food chain, I will ask who reports to them and who do they work alongside. I make contact with these people to confirm I am chasing the right person after all.

Tip 14

Dear Sales Doctor,

Do you believe in going the extra mile for your clients and if so, how do I demonstrate this?

Many people in sales, customer services or any role which involves dealing with customers, talk about 'going the extra mile'. To begin with, I used to think that sounded great, and gave your client the perception that you were going above and beyond for them and were willing to 'go the extra mile' to make them happy.

It wasn't until recently, where I assured a client I would be 'going the extra mile' to which he replied by saying, "Shouldn't you be going the extra mile for me anyway?"

It really made me stop and think and understand things from his perspective. I now tell all my clients that 'the extra mile is our starting point' and it's an ethos that all my staff have bought into and deliver on to the delight of my customers.

"If you care at all,
you'll get some results.
If you care enough,
you'll get incredible results."

Jim Rohn

Tip 15

Dear Sales Doctor,

Is it true you should treat people how you want to be treated?

Many people often refer to that common phrase 'Treat people how you want to be treated'. I disagree with this immensely for one main reason.

As a business owner, I purchase from many suppliers, whether it's for my website, marketing activities, recruitment agencies etc. and as a customer, I am a very laid-back, understanding customer, who requires minimal or no support. I wish all my clients were like me; however, some of them are the exact opposite, therefore if I treated them how I want to be treated, it would cause issues and I'd have some very unhappy customers.

So I have amended this saying to 'Treat people how **they** want to be treated'; this way, I am able to adapt to the clients' needs and provide them with the support that **they** want, as opposed to what I'd be happy with.

"One of the most sincere forms of respect is actually listening to what another has to say."

Bryant H. McGill

Tip 16

Dear Sales Doctor,

I recently started my sales career, and at first I enjoyed it – there's nothing like closing your first sale, it feels amazing.

However, as I have increasingly felt the pressure of meeting targets to hit commission, the other guys have encouraged me to do whatever it takes to make a sale. 'Whatever it takes' here really means lying or exaggerating about the product to get a client on board. I am not sure how comfortable I feel about this. Is telling a little white lie just part and parcel of being a salesman? If everyone else is doing it, should I be doing it too?

Under no circumstances should you lie, no matter how big or small; you will get found out and then all credibility is lost and your company's reputation is damaged. Part of being an exceptional sales professional is finding out your clients' real needs and then highlighting the relevant benefits of your product or service around THEIR needs in the most favourable light possible.

I would change the word 'exaggerate' to 'passion'; there is never a downside to speaking passionately about your offering and if you can back up your claims with case studies, then even better. If you can't, do not lie or exaggerate; again, you will get found out. On occasions I may say to a prospect I am speaking with X company, which gives the impression I am dealing with them; however, the truth is I am simply speaking to them about a project or trying to work with them; they are yet to choose me so I haven't lied, I just haven't elaborated – there's a difference!

Rather than lie to try and win more business, invest your time and energy on analysing how you have won business and do more of that! If it's by going on meetings, then make more prospecting calls and therefore attend more meetings.

If you are winning business, have low conversion rates, then look at what you need to tweak to improve your conversion rates. Ask one of your top performers if you can attend a meeting with them to see what they might be doing differently to you.

I would suggest emailing the prospects where you have lost the deal to ask for detailed feedback. Say, "I am always looking to develop and improve and any feedback would be sincerely appreciated."

Equally, do this for customers that you have won against your competition and email them asking, "So I can learn from this experience, can you please share with me the main reasons you chose me over anybody else you saw?" The knowledge you gain from both these exercises will win you more business in the future.

Normally it's the little things that make the big difference, so focus on what little things you can change to meet and hopefully exceed your targets. If you are unsure, ask your sales manager for advice. Alternatively, I'd be only too happy to help. My details are in the front of this book.

"A wise man can learn more
from a foolish question
than a fool can learn
from a wise answer."

Bruce Lee

Tip 17

Dear Sales Doctor,

What general tips would you provide for working towards starting your own business and starting out with very little capital available?

To answer your question, I would first write a detailed business plan, speak to suppliers you will need to use, and get an idea of all the costings involved.

Then call some of your future competitors acting as a fake customer to get copies of their proposals and understand their pricing models.

Once you have gained a good understanding of the business opportunity, I would establish what starting capital you ACTUALLY need and approach your local bank. Many banks are happy to lend small loans based on the business opportunity and the forecasts of the business.

Alternatively, seek a small investment from your friends and their connections.

The Job Centre offer funding for graduates who are looking at setting up a business, where they offer a small loan to help.

I would recommend attending the start-up exhibition that is held annually as this will give you some inspiration.

"An objection is
not a rejection;
it is simply
a request for
more information."

Bo Bennett

Tip 18

Dear Sales Doctor,

My team and I are very good at closing business but we keep getting stuck on the same objection. "I can't advertise now because I'm working at full capacity and I can't take on anymore business". I normally use the tactic of explaining that they can use our magazine to push a different product or the most profitable services they do, enabling them to cherry-pick the work they're taking on. Unfortunately, that rarely works. Any advice?

This could be viewed as a condition, as opposed to an objection. This means if it's genuine and the company have no intention of growing or taking on additional resource to support their growth, then there really is nothing you can do. I would accept this is a company you cannot work with for the next few months and keep in touch to see what changes.

However, before giving up, there are some key questions I'd ask to see if they are using this objection as a way of getting rid of you or they are telling the truth. My questioning would be as follows:

1. As you are at full capacity at present, what is your appetite for growing your business to the next level?

2. If you wish to grow, what plans have you got in place to generate new business?

3. If happy at working at full capacity, approximatively how many clients make up all of your current business?

4. Out of all those clients, how many contribute to the larger percentage of your revenue?

5. What would you do if you lost those major clients?

6. What is your contingency plan if those major clients decided to leave you and work with your competition?

By asking these questions, it should help you gain more information to confirm their real situation and depending on their responses, you will create an opportunity.

False
Evidence
Appearing
Real

Tip 19

Dear Sales Doctor,

We are a relatively new company selling corporate merchandise and have only been around for just under a year. Many prospective customers are saying they are uncomfortable using us, because of the fear of the unknown. Any ideas how we can overcome this?

When you talk about how good you are, it's bragging; when someone else talks about how good you are, it's proof! Therefore, you need to use testimonials to reassure your prospect and put their mind at rest. Wherever you can, you need to use a relevant testimonial to the prospect. So when I target estate agents for my sales training, I use a testimonial from an estate agent that I am confident they'd have heard of and it talks about how my sales training helped their business i.e. increased the number of viewings the negotiators make, improve their conversions from a viewing to a sales or let, developed their cold calling skills to call landlords and increase the number of valuations they generate.

The more specific the testimonial, the better, so if your client is able to specify by what percentage you increased their business, or reduced their costs etc., the better. When you ask your client for a testimonial, they often agree to it; however, it's never a top priority of theirs and there's nothing in it for them to write it for you. I recommend you suggesting to your client that you will write the testimonial and email it to them for their approval; therefore saving them time and hassle. Ask them for copies of their logo when they approve it, and make sure you get your client's permission for using their testimonial to show your prospective customers. Here is an example of one I use when targeting the hotel industry:

"We were very impressed with the professionalism and enthusiasm that the Sales Doctor brought to the table. All our delegates thoroughly enjoyed the training and it is making a huge difference to our business. The creativity, motivation and attention to detail by the trainers transformed a difficult subject into something enjoyable and commercially successful. We will certainly be using the Sales Doctor in the future."

Stuart Leckie – Head of sales, Jury's Inn

With the growing popularity of social media, it will be great to get some video testimonials from your clients as well.

Prepare them on the sort of things they should say and record them for two minutes talking about how you helped them and their business.

You can then send your prospective clients links to the testimonials, such as: http://youtu.be/kRd9UfdFGlw.

Tip 20

Dear Sales Doctor,

I sell IT software and I have been working on this prospective customer for about four months and they raised an objection about whether our software can do a certain function. I visited them again and took my IT director to demonstrate this functionality and then when I went to close them, they said that they "need to meet with another vendor before making a decision". I feel like I did everything I could to win the business; am I missing something?

This is extremely frustrating when you do everything you can to win the business, and it's still not enough. However, rest assured, there is a great technique that I would recommend here that will stop this from happening again. It's called 'Isolate the objection'. So next time a prospect raises an objection towards what you believe to be the end of the sales cycle, say to the prospect, "Is this the only thing stopping us moving forward?" and remember to close your mouth and enjoy the silence. If the prospect umms and urrs after this question, then you must ask what else do you need to do to win their business? In your situation, they would have mentioned seeing another vendor, so you need to find out who and what you're being compared against and then ask what will they be basing their decision on? This will help you highlight how you are the right choice for them.

If the prospect replies yes, then you reply, "That's great!" and you can use a trial close if you feel it's necessary i.e. "So once I've demonstrated our software has that functionality, you'll be ready to go ahead, is that right?"

"I don't like
that man.
I must get to
know him better."

Abraham Lincoln

Tip 21

Dear Sales Doctor,

I meet so many different types of people in my sales meetings; some I just really connect with and others I don't. Is there any advice you can offer with the ones that I just don't click with?

I had exactly the same challenge when I sold IT software many years ago. The person I normally met with was an IT director or IT manager and sometimes an FD would get involved as well; no matter how hard I tried to have a conversation about things outside of work, to try and build a rapport, it never seemed to work and I really struggled to find that connection.

A couple of years later, I was introduced to a behaviour matrix model by Carl Jung, the Swiss psychotherapist and psychiatrist, which explains how people's behaviour can be placed into one of four quadrants whom all share similar traits. People like to deal with people like them, therefore once you understand a person's behaviour, your job as a sales professional is to adapt your behaviour around theirs.

This makes them more comfortable and you will build rapport on their level, not yours. In my book, Coffee's for Closers, I explain this in much further depth and you will learn how to identify their behaviour by a variety of ways like the look of their office, the words they use, their body language etc. and most importantly, how to adapt around them.

The other thing I can suggest to find a connection when out on meetings is to use a technique called matching, which comes from NLP (Neuro Linguistic Programming).

As the name suggests, you match the person's body language, so if they have their legs crossed, you cross their legs, and if they are leaning forward, then you do the same.

Equally, match their tone of voice, their pace of speech, the language they use etc.

By matching them discreetly, you will again make them more comfortable and they will be more receptive to your suggestions and ideas.

"Put your money into land. They're not making it anymore."

Abraham Lincoln

Tip 22

Dear Sales Doctor,

I sell investment property in the UK and find it very difficult to really understand what the investor is looking to achieve out of their investment. I ask the question, "What are you looking to achieve from your investment?" They always respond with, "A return on investment", and I don't know how to get them to elaborate. Any suggestions?

Every investor is looking to get a return on the investment in some form of another and some will be more risk averse than others; so your job as their broker is to find out what their true goals and aspirations are and only then are you able to recommend the right investment for them. There are two ways to identify these and one is questioning their past investments and the other is what I call the fast forward question.

So I would start by telling them your job is to understand their strategies and aspirations, and in order to do that, you have a few questions you need to ask. Ask the following:

- What investments have they done in the past?
- If they have invested, you need to find out what they invested in and why.
- What were their expectations and how did those investments perform for them?
- How do they feel about the investments they made?

Now if they haven't invested before and therefore may be slightly nervous and understandably cautious, I would use the fast forward question: "Let's fast forward 12 months from now; how will you know it was the right investment for you?"

Now whatever is their immediate response will be the real driver and motivation behind the investment; so you can expect the following sort of responses:

- I am getting the rental yields you have promised, which has given me peace of mind
- I have been able to release some equity from the property, which has enabled me to invest in other property and build a portfolio
- I have gained more capital appreciation than I expected
- I have not lost any money on the deal
- The whole process has been a lot less hassle than I expected

Whatever response they say, I would respond by saying, "That's interesting, can I ask why is that important to you?" This probing question will allow the investor to elaborate even further and confirm their real drivers.

It's important to record this information and refer back to their real drivers on every correspondence, as this will build the value and confirm with the investor you really understand them and are interested in them. In turn, they will be more comfortable with you and be more receptive to your recommendations.

Tip 23

Dear Sales Doctor,

I work in retail selling kitchens and bedrooms, and find it very difficult to engage a customer when they first walk into store. I always ask if they'd like a drink and 9 out of 10 times, they refuse, so I leave them be. I then find it difficult to approach them again as I feel like I'm pestering them. Is there a way around this?

Customers are quite defensive these days and are almost expecting staff to pounce on them; so their natural reaction is to refuse a drink and be dismissive. Naturally, this puts you on the back foot and understandably you feel awkward to re-approach.

The key is to always look busy, but approachable. I recommend having a cloth in your back pocket so as soon as you see a customer walk into store, you can start cleaning the surfaces. You must acknowledge them immediately by a simply "Good morning/afternoon".

After approximately 45 seconds, I suggest approaching them and introducing yourself and saying the following: "I'm just making myself a coffee; what would you like? Tea or coffee?"

By asking it this way, I guarantee you'll get more customers agreeing to a drink, therefore resulting in staying in store for longer and more receptive to discuss their requirements.

"One of the best predictors of ultimate success in either sales or non-sales selling isn't natural talent or even industry expertise, but how you explain your failures and rejections."

Daniel H. Pink

Tip 24

Dear Sales Doctor,

I sell conservatories and although my conversation rate is higher than most my team (about 30% of all my meetings turn into sales), I am still always open to ideas to improve this. My biggest challenge is getting the customers over the line to commit and convincing them to spend their money. Are there any techniques you can suggest for this?

Many customers love the idea of having something like a conservatory and when they find out the actual cost, it puts them off and they find it hard to convince themselves.

One technique I would suggest is called 'just pretend'. To take away all the pressure, you say to the customer, "Let's pretend you have gone ahead with the order; how would you design the layout of your new conservatory?"

Let the customer get really enthusiastic about the idea of having bought it and allow them to start visualising it and designing their perfect conservatory. So when it comes to talking about the finance for it, they have already sold it to themselves and find it a lot harder to say no due to the sheer disappointment.

"If you so choose,
the challenges can make
you stronger.
If you so choose,
the disappointments
can make you
more determined."

Ralph Marston

Tip 25

Dear Sales Doctor,

I like sales, once you've built up a decent relationship with your clients, but I can't stand cold calling. I dread it every time I have to do it, and I think sometimes the fact I don't like doing it comes through and has a negative effect on my pitch.

Any suggestions of how I can overcome this fear and get to like cold calling more? Or at least not let my dislike of it affect my sales technique?

I would firstly like to reassure you that you are not alone; at least 90% of sales professionals I have trained, initially felt exactly the same as you. However, once they understood what I am about to share with you and really bought into it, they began to view cold calling very differently and actually enjoy it now, believe it or not!

To become an expert in the art of sales requires discipline, persistence, tenacity and a lot of skill. Part of that skill requires mastering how to cold call and create an opportunity over the phone. The first thing I want you to change is the name 'cold' call; this implies you know nothing about the company you're calling, you're unsure of whom you will be asking for and you are calling on a whim without any preparation. I would always recommend investing at least three minutes looking up the company online to gain some understanding of what they do, which in turn will help you establish how you can help them. You need to identify which person is most likely to be the decision maker and look for that person's name on the website or using the social media site, LinkedIn. By investing that time, it will give you the ammunition you need to start playing the game of what I call 'smart' calling.

I genuinely view smart calling as a GAME; the more you play it, the better you become. Like any game, you are bound to make many mistakes at first; however, as long as you review the game afterwards and identify what you can do differently next time, only then will you start to get better and enjoy it more. The first 10 seconds of the call are the most vital, as you have interrupted the prospect during their working day and they will make a very quick judgement as to whether they want to take the call. This is your small window of opportunity where you need to engage the prospect and tell them something of value that makes them decide it's worth listening further and continuing the conversation with you.

Many salespeople fall into two traps on that initial call. One is they sound miserable and bored and sound like they are expecting a NO before they have even started. This sounds like where you may have been falling into. One quick fix to this is smile when you dial; it's cheesy as hell, although extremely effective. Try sounding monotonous and bored with a big grin on your face. The second trap is salespeople like to bore the prospect with telling them all the facts and features of what their company does and what products they offer.

Most prospects switch off immediately and start to lose the will for that salesperson to live! It's all about explaining to the prospect not what you do, but what you have done, successfully, with people or businesses like theirs. If you are able to name-drop clients that the prospect would recognise, then all the better, as this will build your credibility immediately. Let me illustrate an example of an opening statement I use when I smart call an estate agent about sales training.

"Good morning, Mr Agent, thanks for taking my call. My name is Tony Morris from the Sales Doctor. Are you familiar with my business?"

Answer: No

"To make you aware, we have successfully delivered sales training with many agents like A and B which has helped double the number of viewings they make, in some cases, triple their conversion rates, and provided innovative techniques to help them gain new landlords details.

"To see if we can help you, can I ask now do you develop your negotiators?"

As you can see, by using this opening gambit, it creates curiosity and gains the prospect's interest immediately. The more you practise your opening statement and develop your questioning skills, the more success you will have. Like any game you play, the better you start to do and the more you win, the more you enjoy it.

On your next day of smart calling, not cold calling, prepare your opening statement and go win that appointment or sale and let me know how you feel differently afterwards.

"I feel that luck is preparation meeting opportunity."

Oprah Winfrey

"Always remember
that you are
absolutely unique.
Just like
everyone else."

Margaret Mead

Tip 26

Dear Sales Doctor,

I am an IFA and I generate the majority of my new business by attending networking events. I was at an event the other day and was aware that out of 35 attendees, there were four IFAs. So when someone approached me and asked, "What do you do for a living?" I found it frustrating to reply, "I'm an IFA," as I was not able to differentiate myself from the other three in the room. Any ideas?

If you think about the question, "What do you do?", it could be rephrased to "How do you help people?" When you respond with "I'm an IFA," that's actually telling someone what you ARE, not what you DO.

Next time, someone asks, "What do you do?" reply by telling them how you help people i.e. I help people make the most of their money and give them peace of mind. This response creates curiosity and will entice them to question you further and make you stand out and be memorable.

If someone asks me, "What do you do?" I used to say, "I'm a sales trainer". I now say, 'I help salespeople convert more business and maximise every opportunity".

"People often say
that motivation
doesn't last.
Well, neither
does bathing -
that's why we
recommend it daily."

Zig Ziglar

Tip 27

Dear Sales Doctor,

My sales team really struggle with motivation because the average sales cycle with our products are between two to three years. Do you have any ideas how I, as their sales manager, can keep them motivated?

I have many clients that fall into this category, and the sales manager and sales director have also struggled to keep up morale and motivation within their team. The first thing to appreciate is the reason for the lack of motivation is they are ONLY focusing on the end result, which is the sale at the end of the two or three years. However, there are numerous tasks required throughout the three year duration in order to achieve the sale.

Therefore, I recommend getting your sales consultant to compile a monthly or quarterly plan of exactly what tasks are required to achieve the sale. Therefore, each time they complete a task, they can celebrate that mini win and feel motivated for the next task ahead. Examples of the tasks could be to gain an additional influencer within their prospective client, to arrange a site visit at your premises etc.

The second piece of advice I give my clients is they need to know exactly what motivates and demotivates every member of their sales team. Many of them were aware that their team were money motivated; however, they were unaware of specifically how much they need to earn and most importantly how they wish to spend that money. What I mean by this is if you know your sales consultant is looking to earn £100,000 per annum and he has chosen that figure as he's saving up to buy a property, then it would be good to know exactly how much deposit he requires to save.

By understanding this, you could help motivate the consultant by monitoring what percentage he has earned towards his deposit every month. By having a specific target is always more motivational than just a figure of money.

Depending on your sales team, it is sometimes a good idea to get them to create their own board displaying pictures of their goals i.e. pictures of the car they are looking to buy, the property they are saving towards, the holiday etc. These visual reminders are great ways of motivating your sales team.

"Ability is what you're capable of doing. Motivation determines what you do. Attitude determines how well you do it."

Lou Holtz

Tip 28

Dear Sales Doctor,

I have a team of eight sales consultants and my top performer is quite often 10 minutes late in the morning. I have had words with him in the past and he says it's not affecting his figures and he outperforms the rest of the team, so he can't see the problem. Although I find it frustrating, I find it hard to argue his point and I can't afford to lose him as he contributes around 45% of my team's target every month. Can you help?

It's always dangerous to rely so heavily on an individual salesperson; you have to ask yourself, if he was to hand his notice in tomorrow, would your business go under? If you feel it would make an enormous impact, then you need to develop the rest of your team immediately. You know the saying, "Don't keep all your eggs in one basket"? The same is relevant to your sales team. Rather than focus the majority of your energy on the one salesperson, invest your time and energy on bringing everyone else up to speed.

Now the salesperson can argue that being late doesn't affect his figures. However, you could argue what impact would it make if he was able to make an extra sales call per day, if he was on time like the rest of your team.

Equally, it's imperative to get across to him that you expect ALL your staff to be in by a certain time and why should he be an exception to the rule. Just because he performs well doesn't give him the right to have special treatment. It's not one rule for him and one rule for others, otherwise it would be mayhem and no one would know what rules must be adhered to.

There are three ways I suggest on how to handle this individual sales consultant. Firstly, you need to explain to him that to be a professional sales consultant requires more than just good figures. You need to be punctual, you need to take pride in your appearance, you need to have a positive attitude and you need excellent knowledge of your products and the marketplace.

Therefore, in order to develop him, you need to help him with his time keeping and see what is required to ensure he is always on time. I would question why he struggles with his punctuality and perhaps you can offer your support to help him. Maybe he's having personal issues at home that he doesn't wish to divulge?

Secondly, you can get his buy-in by explaining that as the top performer of the team, the rest of the sales team look up to him and he therefore is the benchmark. Therefore, it's crucial that he leads by example, which means he is always on time as well as adhering to all the other areas I mentioned earlier.

The third and final idea on how some of my clients have handled this challenge is to put the problem onto the salesperson. Say to him, "If you were in my position as the sales manager, how would you handle this situation?" By doing this, it gets the salesperson to think of it from a different person's perspective and offer his own advice. Sometimes people are more inclined to listen to their own advice, rather than their boss' advice.

Tip 29

Dear Sales Doctor,

Since the recession, I'm finding the majority of my prospects negotiating on my price and I am getting the feeling unless I concede and reduce my costs, I will stop winning any new business. Any ideas?

You are not alone and companies are tightening their belts. However, that doesn't mean you have to drop your prices every time. In fact, I would be suggesting staying strong and be proud of your price. One major reason prospects ask for a discount is because you haven't demonstrated value. Imagine walking into the glamorous Ritz Hotel in London and asking, "How much is it to stay the night?" and they reply, "£450 per night." How do you think they would respond if you ask, "How much can I have off then?" I am pretty confident they would give you a look of shock and disgust and reply by saying, "This is the Ritz, Sir. We don't offer discounts". Why should you be any different about your products and services?

Now if you push the Ritz further and explain you planned on staying there for a week and insist on a discount, I am sure they would offer you a complimentary afternoon tea or dinner. However, no money has been discounted and they have kept you happy. So to be best prepared for every meeting, I would recommend having a few things you can trade in as an alternative for discounting your price.

Depending on your product or service, here are a few things you can think about: payment terms, after sales support, technical help, delivery costs etc. Ultimately you want to give away something that has a big perceived value to your customer and minimal value to yourself, whilst remembering to keeping a good poker face and hiding this fact.

Tony Morris

It's important to remember when entering a negotiation that you're not looking to win, as that will come across that you are there to do battle. No one likes to lose, so if you win, how receptive would your customer be to move forward?

The aim is for you both to win and both get what you want out of the deal to move forward.

"What is a cynic?
A man who knows
the price of everything
and the value
of nothing."

Oscar Wilde

Tip 30

Dear Sales Doctor,

I am an excellent salesperson, if I do say so myself, when I'm talking to the decision maker. But my biggest problem is actually getting to speak to the right person. I often come up against secretaries, receptionists and PAs who have a God complex. These Rottweilers seem to see it as their job to keep their boss from having to talk to anyone, and are fiercely protective. It is extremely frustrating. I know if I actually got the chance to talk to the key person, there's a good chance I'd make the sale. Any tips on how to get past these jobsworth guardians so you can talk to the one in charge?

The amusing thing is these gatekeepers, or Rottweilers, as you call them, have been trained to stop salespeople getting through.

Most salespeople are under the impression they have to speak to them in a certain way, normally with no respect, and that will get past them. This could not be further from the truth. So the first thing is to treat them like a human being, and ask for their help and they'll normally, not always, respond positively. Be as friendly, charming and sincere as you can and you might shock yourself!

One very common objection a gatekeeper may give you is, "no name policy". Therefore, if you haven't got the contact's name, they can't put you through. With the genius invention of LinkedIn, that has eliminated 80% of these cases. Type into LinkedIn the name of the company and then there is a tab for employees; it will provide a few names and if your chosen contact isn't there, then call up and say, "I have spoken to X and he wasn't the right person; who would you recommend?"

Failing that, here are some great ways to overcome the no name policy:

1. Make up a name. "Good morning, can I speak to Mike Beard please?"

"We don't have a Mike Beard here."

 I have him down as the sales director. Who has taken over his position?"

2. "Hi, it's Tony here from Yell.com and I am just updating my records. Is Mike Beard still the sales director? He's not, who's taken over his role? Great, can I just get his email address and mobile, please, for my data?"

3. Go on their website. There will usually be a name mentioned somewhere on the 'Meet the Team or 'In the News pages. It might not be the contact you are after. However, you can use that name when you call back.

4. Be aware of the times to call. If you do have the director's names but the gatekeeper won't put you through, call during times the gatekeeper is unlikely to be there, such as before 08:45am, between 12:15 – 13:45, and after 17:30.

5. Make a joke of the no name response. This must be done with charm and wit, or you will get called a variety of rude names like I have in the past. So when the gatekeeper says, "I'm afraid it's a no name policy," simply respond, "I understand that, and sorry, who am I speaking with?"

"Michelle" she replies. "Ah! I think you may have just broken your policy, Michelle!" I normally get a good one d**khead and the lovely sound of a dead phone line; however, it's worked on occasion.

6. Gatekeepers are trained to ask, "Are they expecting your call?" Your response must always be, "I'm returning their call."

7. If you have the contact name and the gatekeeper asks, "Is this a cold call or a new business call?" repond with, "No, I am returning their call." Always ask for your contact by their first name, as this gives the impression you know them personally.

Tip 31

Dear Sales Doctor,

I'm finding so many prospects I call on are saying they're 'happy with current supplier' and I just don't know where to go with it. Any ideas?

This is a very common objection that many sales professionals face and it may well be very true that the prospect is happy. However, there is what I call the 'three bites of the cherry approach' that normally creates an opportunity.

The first step is to try and identify pain. Many salespeople ask, "Are you happy with your supplier?" or, "Is there anything you feel they could improve upon?" These terrible closed questions do NOT get the prospect thinking and allows them to reply "No" without giving it any real thought. I always recommend the following questions:

- In your valued opinion, what areas do you feel your current supplier could improve?

- If you had to rate the level of service your current supplier provides on a scale of 1 - 10, 10 being exceptional and 1 being awful, where would you rate them? When they say 8, reply "Okay, what would make them a 10?"

- If there was one thing that would make you even consider looking elsewhere, what would it be?

These leading open questions provoke the prospect to really think about their supplier and come up with areas for improvement, which will enable you to explain how your product or service can help them.

On the rare occasion the prospect is ecstatic with their supplier and they can't think of any areas of improvement, then you move to step two of the approach called 'Review'. You need to ask how long they've been working with their current supplier. No matter what length of time they respond with, you reply, "That's quite a long time and I'm sure you're aware there have been many changes in the marketplace. When did you last review to ensure you are receiving the best quality of product/ service, the best level of service and paying the RIGHT price?"

Now it's possible the prospect has reviewed and if so, you say, "You're clearly an astute individual. Who did you review against and what criteria did you use to benchmark against?" If they haven't reviewed, then you insist on them benchmarking their current supplier against your offering to either give them ease of mind that what they have is the best for them or that you can add value.

Finally, it leads me to step three, 'The Back-up Plan'. You say to the prospect, "if your current supplier was to let you down or couldn't work within a short lead time or was unable to provide a specific product or service, who would you then look at?" Most companies are unlikely to have a back-up supplier, so if they reply that they have never needed once, I would say, "I appreciate that. However, surely it's better to be prepared if the need arises. I suggest I come and demonstrate our products/ services to ensure we are right for your business and then if the need arises, we'll be able to react immediately."

By using this 'three bites of the cherry approach', it will help you work with most companies that are happy with their current supplier.

Tip 32

Dear Sales Doctor,

My boss keeps telling me listening is the most important part of selling and he says I talk far too much. Is he right about the listening part and what can you suggest to improve this, as I'm evidently not good at it?

Your boss is right and the reason being is people love to talk about themselves; their business, their problems or challenges, their personal life etc. and if we are talking, than we are NOT listening to them.

An Italian economist called Vilfredo Pareto created a law which was aptly named 'Pareto's Law' which is known as the 80/20 rule. It's been proven that in a retail environment, 80% of profits comes from 20% of their products, and in an office environment, 80% of productivity normally comes from 20% of the staff. The same goes to sales; when you are speaking on the phone and/or face-to-face, you should be aiming to speak just 20% and listening 80%. I am sure you have heard the expression, "You have two ears and one mouth, use them accordingly."

So how do we develop our listening skills? It's easy to say just listen more, but in reality that doesn't fix everyone's problem, as some people are much better listeners than others. They are what are referred to as auditory people and their brains are programmed differently to those who struggle to listen. However, there are three techniques I can recommend that will make an enormous difference to your listening skills:

1. Use the tag on questioning technique. If someone says, "I love Chinese food," reply by asking, "What's your favourite Chinese dish?" This will improve your conversational ability and your listening skills at the same time.

2. Summarise your conversations to ensure you haven't missing anything. At the end of a meeting or a conversation say, "To ensure I haven't missed anything, I just want to summarise what you've told me; a,b,c,d, Was there anything else you'd like to add?"

3. Recap and reframe in your words. As you are having a conversation, jump in at appropriate intervals and say, "So what you are basically saying to me is ...." This will help you digest the information and again ensures you have heard the person correctly.

Listening skills is like a muscle; the more you work on it, the stronger it becomes. Therefore, to begin with, you may find it challenging, but as the weeks go on, you will improve dramatically.

"I like to listen. I have learned a great deal from listening carefully. Most people never listen."

Ernest Hemingway

Tip 33

Dear Sales Doctor,

Last week, I received a very good lead which came via a Facebook group. The prospective client posted a request on a group for mums asking if anyone could recommend a loft conversion company. Young and growing families who are short of space are our target market. Our name popped up several times, amongst other firms, and she made contact by email. I responded immediately and booked an appointment – she lives around the corner and I was able to walk round. I went suited and booted and arrived on time.

The meeting went well and there was excellent rapport – until she asked how much the work would cost to convert the loft into a master bedroom with en-suite. I told her that I would be sending a written quote, but as an indication it would be in the region of £35,000 to £40,000. At that point the smiles went, faces looked like stone and the atmosphere went cold. "What do you think about the price?" I said. She replied, "We've been quoted anything from £25,000 to £30,000." Feeling somewhat on the back foot and defensive, I explained the benefits of our company again but this was seemingly falling on deaf ears.

I resigned myself to the fact that price was going to be the driving force behind their decision and unless I could come close to their expectations, I was not going to win the work. I told them that we had carried out some excellent conversions locally and I would be happy to arrange viewings in due course. Within a few days, I had prepared them a written quote and they emailed me back to ask if I could arrange the viewings of completed lofts.

I have to say that I felt reluctant to do so as, at this point, they had not even considered my proposals. I decided to say that I would make the appointments to view only once they'd properly considered my quote.

I don't know if this was the right thing to say as I felt it would perhaps put their backs up – but I didn't want them to use me and my clients to get ideas about loft layouts/finishes etc. when I had no commitment from them that they would proceed. I suppose this goes with the territory but my email did flush them out as they replied saying that my price was "significantly more than the others". I do not believe they have any intention of using my company but I am going to respond setting out the reasons why we are more expensive (members of RICS, FMB, long guarantees etc.) but before doing so, I would be very grateful for your views on this as it's not the first time I've been unable to win clients over due to price.

Regarding your question, let me ask you; do you feel what you were quoting for the job was fair?

Do you feel the other quotes they were given were fair?

Were you genuinely providing them with more for your quote?

If you feel you were offering more than the competition at a fair price, then there is nothing else you could have done and you have to walk away. Alternatively, rather than just drop your price, maybe you could take parts of your offering out and then deduct that from the price?

In truth, you can't win them all and I think you were right to stay strong and justify the reasons why you charge what you do. I would email them a nice message wishing them the best of luck on the job and offering them any assistance in the future should they have any issues.

Ensure this doesn't come across as sour grapes, instead one of genuine support. We both know if someone can do the job at £10k cheaper, they will be cutting corners and making mistakes. Therefore, if you leave the door open, hopefully they'll come back anyway.

Tip 34

Dear Sales Doctor,

I know a good way to get business is word of mouth; however, I don't know how to ask for referrals and when the right time to ask is. Any suggestions?

You are absolutely correct. Referrals are the most effective ways to generate new business. Let me answer your latter question regarding timing. Most people are under the impression they can only ask CLIENTS for referrals, which I strongly disagree with; what about the hundreds of prospects we speak to every week? They say every person knows 1,000 people; with the growth in social media sites likes Facebook and LinkedIn, this is very realistic.

Therefore, when you come across a prospective customer that you are unable to help for whatever reason say to them, "Who could you recommend, such as clients, suppliers or previous places of work, that you feel could benefit from what we do?" If you don't ask, you don't get, so therefore you have nothing to lose.

The best people to ask for referrals are happy customers and if dealt with correctly, they could become your best ever salespeople. So once you've done a great job, arrange a meeting with your client and ask them the following question: "Are you happy with both the service and products we provide you?" You wouldn't be asking this unless you know you are getting a yes! Once the client confirms they are happy, reply by saying, "The majority of my business comes from recommendations and I would sincerely appreciate if you could be so kind as to introduce me to a couple of people you deal with that you feel could also benefit from the products/ services I offer. With that in mind, who comes to your mind?"

They key is to ask the question. However, there are other ways you can ask it below. Just choose whichever you are most comfortable with:

1.   "Can I ask you, Mr Client, if we swapped jobs tomorrow, who would be the first three people you'd call?"

2.   "If we were in the pub and your mate walked in, would you introduce me? (Assuming you get a yes) Great with that in mind..."

The reason referrals are so powerful and effective is because people are heavily persuaded by people they trust. Therefore, when someone they trust tells them all about the great experience they have had in working with YOU and benefiting from YOUR products/ services, you are 80% there.

Therefore, in future every inbound enquiry you receive, the first question you should ask the prospect is, "Who recommended you to my company?" Not only does this provide you with the source of the enquiry, it also gives the impression that you receive many recommendations.

Tip 35

Dear Sales Doctor,

I am a very positive person and I always look on the bright side of life; my glass is always half full!

However, in the past few months I moved into a new job selling printers and am really struggling. I'm working really hard and doing all the things I used to when I was selling data in my last job, but in the past 10 meetings, I have only managed to covert three of them and I can't help getting down. What can you recommend to help pick me back up?

Rest assured you wouldn't be human if you didn't get frustrated or down by losing business; this clearly shows you are passionate about what you do and are hungry to be a success, which speaks volumes about your determination. The fact you monitor and measure your conversation rates is also a positive, as you clearly are receptive to personal development.

So what I would recommend you change is how you are viewing things. I read something quite recently by a great motivational speaker called Richard Denny, who said, "You win some, you learn some, but you never lose some!" I agree with this entirely and I'm an advocate for the fact there is no such thing as failure, it's all feedback. So rather than view it as you lost seven deals, change that to" I learned seven new lessons that will help me win more business in the long run." Equally focus on what you did gain from these meetings or presentations, as opposed to what you didn't gain. Would it be fair to say you're better at presenting the 10th time, rather than your 1st attempt?

You have gained new prospects for your pipeline and built rapport with new contacts who know other people that they could refer you too, if YOU ask!

The key is to gain feedback. If you don't already, I would strongly recommend you create an email template and call the subject line 'Your valued feedback'. In the email, write the following:

I appreciate you have not chosen to use my products or services at this juncture and I wish you the best of luck with the route you have chosen.

I am always looking to learn, grow and develop, so with that in mind, can you be so kind to provide me with your honest feedback as to why you decided not to progress with me at this stage. I will not take any offence to your comments whatsoever, quite the contrary, as I will use them to improve myself for next time.

I really appreciate your time in providing me with your comments and if I can be of any further assistance in the future, please get in touch. I will diarise to call you in the next few weeks to see how things panned out for you.

Warmest Regards

Tony

Tip 36

Dear Sales Doctor,

I am in new business sales and I really struggle where to get leads from. Are there any places you can recommend?

Prospecting is an important part of the sales process and one that requires a lot of time. However, what is very important is you are focusing on the right type of business. I would recommend looking at the clients you have acquired or that your company have won and identify which industries or types of company is your perfect customer. Only then can you know the type of lead you should be looking for.

Every meeting I attend, I like to build rapport with the prospect and one of the best ways of doing this is to get them talking about themselves. One question I often ask is how long have you been working here and where were you working previously? Firstly, this shows a real interest in the prospect and secondly, it generates some leads for you to call afterwards. Depending on how the meeting went and the level of rapport you built, you could say to the prospect, "You mentioned you previously worked at IBM. Who could you recommend I speak to there about how I can help them?"

Another good question to show an interest and generate leads is to ask the prospect, "Which companies do you normally come up against in a tender?" Again, the next two or three companies the prospect shares are more leads for you to call.

If you are out selling in the field, it's imperative that your time is spent wisely. Let's say you are based in London and have a new business meeting scheduled for a week's time in Manchester at 15:00.

I would now look to make further two or three meetings around that meeting to make the most of my time. There are some great free websites that allows you to enter an industry and an area to target i.e. IT software vendors in Manchester, and it will provide a listing of numerous companies in and around that area to call. The websites I recommend are:

www.ufindus.com
www.businessmagnet.com
www.freeindex.co.uk
www.yell.com

The final suggestion I have to generate leads is exhibitions. Depending on your target location and target customer, look up venues that hold exhibitions such as NEC in Birmingham, Excel, Olympia and Earls Court in London, GMex in Manchester etc. and look up the calendar of events that are running throughout the year. Choose the exhibition that is most likely to have your target customers exhibiting at and print off the exhibitor list. This will provide you with lists of companies, contact numbers and potentially a contact name.

Tip 37

Dear Sales Doctor,

One of the biggest challenges I face as a salesperson is that there are not enough hours in the day. What advice can you give me on time management?

It's one of the things I get asked the most and it's one of the toughest things to get right; the truth is, it's all about discipline.

I am sure you have heard the saying "Work smarter, not harder". Well this is imperative to effective time management. However, what it doesn't tell you is how can we work smarter?

The first thing I'd recommend is carrying out a time log. For one week, make a note of every single thing you are doing every day and record a time next to it. At the end of the day, calculate how much time are you proactively spending on generating sales because without this, your job is redundant! You can then identify what tasks you are doing that perhaps you could delegate or carry out at different times of the day.

One thing that is fixed is the times that you are able to make sales calls: 09:15am to 12:30, and 13:30 to 17:00. Therefore, I would recommend carrying out any other tasks outside of these times, where possible.

Many clients I train write to-do lists and some of them actually do the tasks; however, it's crucial that you prioritise the list. When prioritising, it's not what you'd like to do first, it's what needs to be done first.

When working in an office, you will come across what I call time thieves and it takes great discipline to avoid these at all costs. The three biggest time thieves are emails, meetings for the sake of meetings and your peers.

When making sales calls, I recommend blocking out power hours to be on the phone and closing your laptop to avoid the temptation of looking at your emails and being disturbed.

If there are meetings going on that you are asked to attend and you believe they are not crucial, don't be afraid of asking if it's absolutely crucial that you attend. Explain your urgent workload and the time you have available to complete it and a reasonable manager should agree your absence.

Finally when your peers or members of staff approaches you, say to them "I have a,b,c to complete by such a time. Unless it's life threatening, do you mind if we discuss this at 14:00?" Provide them with a specific time which should avoid you coming across as rude.

Try all these things and I guarantee you'll have more time on your hands. Now stop reading this and get back to work!

Tip 38

Dear Sales Doctor,

I am proficient at closing budget when my leads are properly pre-qualified. However, I struggle with the, "I haven't got any budget" objection. How can I overcome this?

In the current climate, this is an objection that arises time and time again. However, what needs to be identified is this; is it true?

The best way to handle this objection is to do what I call the 'side stepping technique' and you say this, "Putting budget to one side, can I ask you...." Now the questions you ask all depends on what you are selling, but the objective is to build the value in the prospect's mind to build the desire for your product/ services. Let me illustrate this. I sell sales training, so once I hear we have no budget, I reply, "Putting budgets to one side, how are you currently developing your salespeople? What areas do you feel they could improve? How many of your team are not achieving their targets?" These questions build the value in the prospect's mind and then I organise a meeting to discuss training; 80% of those never mention budget again as I have demonstrated the value I can bring to their business.

Another method to handle this objection is what I call the 'let's pretend technique' and it goes like this. "Mr Prospect, let's pretend you had a budget for my product/service. Are you happy with what we have discussed today?" If they answer no to this, then you know the budget is not the real objection and you can ask them what is causing them to hesitate. If, on the other hand, they reply positively, then you need to qualify when their budget will next become available. You are then in a position to gain their commitment and potentially negotiate payment terms to fit in around their budget.

"Always be nice
to secretaries.
They are the
real gatekeepers
in the world."

Anthony J. D'Angelo

Tip 39

Dear Sales Doctor,

How do I handle the gatekeeper who wants to know exactly why I'm calling before putting me through?

Funnily enough, the answer to this question is one word you used in your question; handle. Many people talk about getting past the gatekeeper, but in your situation, it's all about handling the gatekeeper. Now in most cases, the gatekeeper will not have the knowledge or authority to be able to answer your question or make a decision; however, they are still a human being and should be treated with respect to not alienate them.

One great technique to handle the gatekeeper is to ask for their help. Many people love to help others when asked; it gives them a feeling of satisfaction knowing they are able to help you in some way. So I recommend it's delivered in this way:

Gatekeeper: Good morning, IBM.

Me: "Yes, good morning. My name is Tony Morris calling from the Sales Doctor. Sorry, who am I speaking with, please?

Gatekeeper: Michelle

Me: Good morning, Michelle, I really hope you can help me. The person I normally speak to in a company of your size is the Head of Learning and Development. Who would that be in your organisation, please?

Gatekeeper: What's the reason for the call?

Me: We have recently been working with companies in your marketplace, training and developing the sales teams to improve performance levels. To answer your question, the reason for my call is to see if we can do the same for you. Who would you suggest, Michelle, would be the ideal person to speak to who would make decisions on developing the sales team?

Now I cannot guarantee this approach works every time, I'll be lying if I said it did. However, it will work more often than not and as long as you remain professional and polite and ask for the gatekeeper's help, you'll be surprised at the results it will bring.

"Effective communication
is 20% what you know
and 80% how
you feel about
what you know."

Jim Rohn

Tip 40

Dear Sales Doctor,

How do I deal with the prospect who, as soon as I sit down, says, "Right, what have you got to show me? Why should I be seeing you, as your guy cold called me?"

I have faced this challenge numerous times and it normally means the telesales person did not qualify the prospect effectively and simply closed him or her just to make an appointment for you. Your job, therefore, is to rebuild the value and create an opportunity.

Your first task is to get the prospect back on your side. To achieve this, you need to demonstrate some value and then ask some great open questions to show a genuine interest in both the prospect and the business. Hopefully, you would have done some preparation prior to the meeting and know about the company; therefore, I would recommend explaining briefly how you have worked with other companies similar to them and what you have helped them achieve.

Once you have found out key information about the prospect's situation, only then are you in a position to show the prospect what he/she needs to see and not a second before.

"Nothing in this world
can take the
place of persistence.
Talent will not:
nothing is more common
than unsuccessful men
with talent.
Genius will not;
unrewarded genius
is almost a proverb.
Education will not:
the world is full of
educated derelicts.
Persistence and determination
alone are omnipotent."

Calvin Coolidge

Tip 41

Dear Sales Doctor,

How do I handle the client who orders then cancels and avoids me?

This is known as buyer's remorse and is quite common in many different sales roles. It usually occurs when not enough value was built during the sales process and once the sale had gone through the salesperson was ambitiously onto the next customer.

They say in sales the first 10 to 15 seconds of a call is the most important; this is equally true of the last 10 to 15 seconds and most salespeople forget this. It's called consolidating the sale.

Once the deal has been agreed, it's imperative that you leave the buyer feeling 100% comfortable of what the next steps are and answer any reservations or concerns they may have. It's vital that you set their expectations of what is happening next and explain clearly that you or someone will be there for them should they have any questions or issues; you can only promise this if it's true and there is an after sales support, or you are setting yourself up for failure.

Be clear to ask the customer if they have any further questions and if there is anything at all they are unsure about or would like you to go over again. Most salespeople avoid asking this as they are scared it will open up a can of worms; however, I'd rather deal with a situation whilst it's in my control, than try and redeem something that is out of my control.

"One secret of success
in life is for a man
to be ready for
his opportunity
when it comes."

Benjamin Disraeli

Tip 42

Dear Sales Doctor,

My boss keeps going on about having the perfect elevator pitch as you never know when an opportunity arises. What advice can you give me to create one?

I think your boss is right and you never know when the right business opportunity will come about. In order to answer your question about creating one, it's important to understand where the name derived from.

It's called an 'elevator pitch' because imagine you are in an elevator and your perfect prospective client walked in and turned to you and said, "So what do you do?" This is one of the most common questions strangers ask each other and you have now been given a maximum time of 15 seconds to tell this stranger about your business with the main objective of creating enough interest and desire that the prospect is keen to find out more.

To help you create your elevator pitch, I would like you to think about this:

- Who would your ideal prospective customer be?

- Now with that ideal customer in your mind, write down one or two things that you feel that customer would gain from working with you. Once you have thought of these two things, you need to put them into a benefit statement. Let me demonstrate what I mean for my business, by answering the question above:

- Who would your ideal prospective customer be?
  An owner of an estate agency that had multiple branches.

- What one or two things would the prospect gain from having my sales training?
  - More stock
  - Increase in profits

My elevator pitch:

I've successfully trained many estate agents helping negotiators cold call private landlords resulting in an increase in stock levels by over 30% which has had a significant impact on their bottom line.

This elevator pitch will create curiosity, desire and an opportunity for me to sit down with my dream prospect and discuss how I can help his/her business.

Tip 43

Dear Sales Doctor,

How do I deal with the customer who is ignoring my calls?

Although it's hard to hear, it sounds like your customer doesn't wish to speak to you if you're being ignored. There are special circumstances where your client is off work due to personal reasons and therefore your call is just not being returned. You need to ask his/her colleagues if this is perhaps the case.

If you ascertain there are no special circumstances and you are being ignored, the next step is to find out why. My advice is to send an email that has the heading: "Have I offended you?" The email would look something like this:

Dear John,

I hope you are well. I am concerned I have done something that has offended or upset you. The last time I spoke to you was on the 15th July where we both discussed............... Since then, I have left numerous messages and sent many emails and have not heard back from you.

I know you are a busy guy, however, after working together successfully for nearly two years, I was hoping for some response and as I said, I am just concerned I have done something that's bothered you.

Please come back to me to let me know and I hope to hear from you soon.

"The risk of
a wrong
decision is
preferable to
the terror
of indecision."

Maimonides

Tip 44

Dear Sales Doctor,

Some of my customers say, "It's not the right time". Is there a way around that?

Although it's extremely frustrating when a customer says that, it also doesn't actually provide you with any real feedback. The key is to find out what the real objection is and if it can be overcome.

You need to choose your words carefully and it all depends on what relationship you have built up with your client. I would recommend saying one of the following below:

- "Clearly I have not done my job properly, because if I had, you would know now is the optimum time to move this forward. Can I ask you where did I get it wrong?"

- "Out of curiosity, what is causing you to hesitate?"

- "It sounds like you have some reservations that I have not covered. What are they?"

"The bottom line is,
when people are crystal
clear about the most
important priorities of
the organization and team
they work with and prioritized
their work around those top
priorities, not only are
they many times more
productive, they discover
they have the time they need to
have a whole life."

Stephen Covey

Tip 45

Dear Sales Doctor,

My customer keeps saying, "It's way down on my priorities." What can I do to raise it to the top of his priorities?

There may be two reasons for this. It's possible you have not built up enough value in your product/service to make it one of your client's priorities. If you feel this is the case, then you need to go back to the beginning and start reconfirming the reasons your client was interested in the first place.

This should involve asking open questions to probe into your client's problems that your product/service were solving in the first place. If you look at this another way, imagine your client had a very ill child and he was told the doctor's surgery was only open for another hour; would getting his child to the doctor's surgery become a priority?

Depending on the level of rapport you have with your client, you may be able to delve into his priorities by asking, "Out of curiosity, what are your other priorities at present?" I would only suggest doing this if you have developed a good relationship with your client, otherwise it could get his back up and he may become quite defensive.

"The healthiest competition
occurs when average
people win by
putting above
average effort."

Colin Powell

Tip 46

Dear Sales Doctor,

I recently had a fantastic meeting and thought the deal was in the bag. The prospect then turned around and said, "I need to see another two suppliers before making a decision." What could I have done differently?

This is really frustrating, especially when you had the feeling the deal was in the bag. The lesson I would take from this is to find out at the beginning, which other companies the prospect is looking at.

Once the prospect shares that, it's imperative to find out what are the prospect's three key priorities when choosing a supplier? Make sure you write down the exact terminology the prospect uses when describing what's important to him, and then use that same terminology back to him in any emails or future dialogue. Let me illustrate how powerful this is.

I had a meeting with a company a few years ago and I found out during the meeting he was looking at my training company and three others, two of whom I was very familiar with.

I then asked what will he base his ultimate decision on. He really opened up and said, "It's crucial the training is **very practical** and **hands-on** so my team can put it straight into practice. He explained his team get very demotivated and he needs the trainer to **boost their morale** and keep them **performing at their optimum level**. He finally shared that it's important the company has experience in his industry, in order to get buy-in from his team.

When I compiled my proposal, I made sure I used the prospect's words that I highlighted in bold. To demonstrate my experience in his industry, I used testimonials and case studies from companies in his industry.

Now I cannot say with 100% certainty that was the only reason I won the business over my competition. However, I know it didn't hurt.

If I have made

an appointment with you,

I owe you punctuality,

I have no right to throw away

your time,

if I do my own.

Richard Cecil

Tip 47

Dear Sales Doctor,

I work for a big hotel group. After four months of getting in front of the key decision maker, he turned around and said, "We used your hotel a year ago and had an awful experience, so he has lost all trust in us." I have no idea how to overcome this. Any ideas?

The first thing to ascertain is, what was this awful experience? By asking this will show interest in the prospect and help you prepare your answer to reassure him/her that things have dramatically changed.

For argument's sake, let's pretend the prospect replies, "I found the staff rude and unhelpful and wouldn't wish to return." Now it's imperative to show real empathy to the prospect and then reassure him/her by explaining how things have improved. The technique is known as the third party proof, as you are using a third party in your story by saying the following:

"I completely understand how you FEEL, we had quite a few guests who stayed around a year ago that FELT exactly the same. What they have now FOUND is all our staff have been through a rigorous training programme and we pride ourselves on delivering world class service. Please come into our hotel for a complementary lunch or dinner, as I'd love to get your valued thoughts and opinions on how you find our staff now. When is the most convenient time for you to come by?

"When you
make a
promise,
keep it."

Zig Ziglar

Tip 48

Dear Sales Doctor,

I am responsible for making appointments for a field sales rep who sells photocopiers and printers. He has trained me to say to the prospect, "I'm in your area on Tuesday, can I see you then?" and I just don't seem to be getting the results. Have you got any better techniques than this?

I am not surprised to hear you're not having much success with this, for the simple reason this is a very old fashioned and cheesy technique that buyers are now aware of. Today's buyers are more switched on and have heard these lines in the past.

Before you make the call, you need to be aware of the location the company is based. Let's pretend the company is based in Salford; you then need to find a city located quite close to that area, like Manchester.

You qualify the prospect and then say the following line: "From what you've kindly shared, we need to meet. I am going to be in Manchester next week; that's close to Salford, isn't it?" Once the prospect says yes, reply with, "Great! Well I am currently available on Tuesday morning and Thursday afternoon next week; which would suit you better?'

By saying you are close by is more believable and by giving two options makes it harder for the prospect to refuse the meeting.

"The best move you can
make in negotiation
is to think of an incentive
the other person
hasn't even thought of -
and then meet it."

Eli Broad

Tip 49

Dear Sales Doctor,

I struggle on negotiating with prospects and normally end up dropping the price. What can I do to avoid having to drop my prices?

Many people go into a negotiation situation and are looking to win; the problem with that in my opinion is you have the mindset that you are going into a battle and are looking to emerge victoriously! Is this a good mindset before potentially starting a new relationship with a client? Not really; who likes to be on the losing side?

Therefore, when I plan to go into a negotiation, my mindset is on building a partnership with my new client and making sure both sides are 100% comfortable in moving forward. One of the first things I do is plan what variables I have to negotiate with, such as payment terms, contract length, delivery schedules, after sales support etc. and therefore I have lots to trade, rather than feeling like I have to drop my price.

The second thing I do is plan the 3 Cs. The first is 'Conquer'; this is what I'd love in an ideal world. The second is 'Compromise'; this is what I'd be happy to accept as a fair negotiation. The third is 'Concede'; this is where I make a decision to accept the prospect's wishes or I walk away. We all need a walk away point, as not every deal is right for both parties.

One major rule to remember when negotiating is never give anything away without getting something back in return, otherwise you are not negotiating, you're just giving things away.

"Nothing can add more
power to your life
than concentrating
all your energies
on a limited set
of targets."

Nido Qubein

Tip 50

Dear Sales Doctor,

For the last three months, I haven't been able to hit my targets and I've completely lost confidence. My colleagues keep telling me to snap out of it but I can't shake off my self-doubt. What shall I do?

This is 100% natural, and in sales you always have peaks and troughs; it's part of the game. The key is how you are viewing the last three months. I am a strong believer that in sales, there is no such thing as failure; it's all feedback. So rather than look at it as what have you lost, view it as what knowledge you have gained - you've learned what's not working and what requires tweaking in your approach.

Equally you would have found some companies that you just can't work with for whatever reason. Although this doesn't help you hit your target, you had to contact these companies at some point; at least they have now been called and you can move on to the next prospects. Therefore, it's not a wasted call; again, it's part of the process.

During the past three months, you would have identified some companies that you may not be able to work with now, although they are now in your pipeline of your activity. You have probably found out who the key decision maker is, which supplier they currently work with, pitfalls with their supplier, contract expiry date, costings etc. The point I'm highlighting is focus on what you have achieved, as opposed to what you have not achieved.

When football managers have a team talk and motivate them, they choose to do this in the trophy room. The reason for this is they like the team to be surrounded by past success.

It's a great reminder that they can do it and have done it! As salespeople, it's important to continuously remind ourselves of our past success and to never forget that. I recommend keeping a record of all our wins, no matter how big or small, so we can look back at these and keep our confidence up.

"It's about listening first, then selling."

Erik Qualman

Tip 51

Dear Sales Doctor,

Sometimes when I know I'm on the brink of getting a deal, I overpromise things to the client, which later comes back to haunt me. Why do I keep doing this? And how can I stop?

I understand why you might do this. Naturally you get excited about being on the brink of closing a deal and therefore if the client asks you anything, you don't want to say anything negative, and that may affect you winning the business.

One of the most important parts of the sales cycle is called 'consolidating the sale'. This is where you outline to the customer everything they are getting as part of the deal, to avoid any 'you said, he said' scenario. Therefore, it's crucial that anything discussed must go in writing, so you can refer to it at a later date, if need be. Equally, you need to ensure the customer is 100% clear on what the next steps are and the time frames they will be delivered in. If you do this at the end of every sale, you will avoid any confusion on both sides and you will not overpromise and underdeliver.

Buyers are aware that when the salesperson is on the brink of winning their business, they are at their most vulnerable and most generous state. Therefore, wise buyers will use this time to try and negotiate additional products or services as part of the deal, without having to pay anymore for it.

It's important to be strong at this point and realise this is just a negotiation tactic, and instead reinforce exactly what the buyer is getting and rebuild the value.

I discuss this in detail in the negotiation chapter in my book 'Coffee's for Closers'.

Where possible, you want to underpromise and overdeliver at the end of the sales process. For example, if you know a product takes three days for delivery, it might be wise to tell the customer they should expect it in five days, so when it arrives two days early, they are impressed. This also gives you some room for error, and again, it avoids any frustration from your customer.

Next time you are on the brink of a sale and that wonderful rush of excitement and adrenalin arises, remember to remain calm and clearly outline what the deals entail. Get agreement from the customer that everything makes perfect sense and you have answered all their questions; then thank them for their business and ask for a referral.

Tip 52

Dear Sales Doctor,

I have been in customer service for as long as I can remember, but I'm considering the move into sales. How can I do this? And what personality do I need to have, or can everything be learnt?

It's an interesting question and something I rarely get asked, as customer services is a different beast to sales. Normally, a person who enjoys dealing with difficult or angry customers and handling complaints is made up of a different make-up to a salesperson. However, saying that, many of the skills required to be successful in customer services are transferable to the sales arena.

So my first question to you is, what has prompted this change? Be sure you know exactly what your reasons are for moving into sales, as this is the first thing that will be asked by any competent sales recruitment consultant. You will need to have a clear and concise answer that will demonstrate your ambition and desire, as opposed to highlighting any negative feelings towards customer services.

You'll need to decide which sales role appeals to you. Would you rather be selling over the phone, or would you prefer to be face-to-face? If it's over the phone, does it appeal to you to be taking inbound calls or would you rather be proactive and making outbound calls?

If you decide face-to-face is what appeals to you, then you need to decide the type of face-to-face sales that is of interest. You can either look at a retail environment that is all business to consumer (B2C) or going out on appointments in a business to business environment (B2B). These decisions should be based on what motivates you, what interests you and, most importantly, where you feel your strengths lie.

To answer your question about what personality you need to have for sales is a difficult question to answer. For the simple reason that people buy people who are like them; therefore, the most successful type of salesperson is like a chameleon and is able to mould or adapt to fit in with their environment. The technique is described as 'matching' or 'mirroring' where you quite literally copy the prospect's behaviour; if they are very direct, then you must act very direct, in order to make them comfortable. Like everything in life, this skill takes time to learn and develop, to come across as natural. However, once you master it, the world is your oyster.

Finally, you asked if everything can be learnt. People have often debated, can you teach someone to sell, or are you just born a natural salespeople? As the owner of Sales Doctor, a successful sales training company, I would be pretty foolish to preach that you cannot teach a person how to sell; however, I would argue that some people are born with what's described as the gift of gab and have a natural gift at persuading and influencing others. That said, I know you can learn the skills and techniques to sell, as I have helped in excess of 3,000 people achieve great things and I assure you they were far from natural. As you have many years of experience in customer services, you will be able to transfer a lot of the skills required over to sales; such as how to empathise, how to persuade and influence, how to take control, how to communicate and, most importantly, how to listen. This is by far one of the most important skills required for salespeople and one the majority of salespeople struggle with, as they love the sound of their own voice and never know when to shut up. If you have been successful in customer services, you have probably mastered the art of listening and therefore will go far.

Tip 53

Dear Sales Doctor,

My boss says I rely on email too much to sell. What's your opinion on whether you can sell on an email?

I'm afraid to say, I agree with your boss. Think about it this way; if it's more effective to sell via email, then sales managers or directors would hire professional copywriters. There was a study conducted by Harvard Business School over a 25 year period on how people communicate and below were their findings:

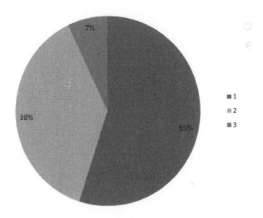

The survey found that the majority of how we communicate is non verbal (body language); and then how we say it makes up 38% of how we communicate. Therefore, if only 7% of how we communicate are with words alone, how can we use email to sell? We cannot possibly get across a message in the same manner on an email as HOW WE SAY IT over the phone.

Equally, we cannot gauge a person's reaction or feedback from an email, whereas over the phone we can hear how they respond to whatever we share.

There is a big difference between what you say and what someone hears; this is amplified on an email, and emails can be read out of context very easily, causing offence. Therefore, to avoid this, pick up the phone and speak to your prospective customer.

Finally, it's much easier to persuade and influence someone over the phone and then you can use emails to reinforce points you have made and use testimonials and/or case studies to back up what you've said.

"I see people putting
text messages on the phone
or computer
and I think,
'Why don't you just call?'"

William Shatner

Tip 54

Dear Sales Doctor,

I sell credit card PDQ terminals to cafes, restaurants and small retail businesses, and all my selling is door knocking. All my confidence is getting knocked out of me because I keep getting rejected. Any ideas?

A big part of why you might be getting a negative reaction, or 'rejected' as you have labelled it, is probably down to two reasons. Number one is how you are delivering your message and the confidence in your approach, and number two is the actual message itself.

Let's start with the message. In my experience, many salespeople doing cold calling, whether that's over the phone or face-to-face, tell the prospect all about themselves and what they do. This is a real no-no, as it only bores the prospect and they will normally dismiss what you are telling them. When working out what to say, you need to look at it from your prospect's perspective and ask yourself this question: what's in it for me? What would the prospect like to hear that would entice them to listening further and then take action; after all, this is our objective, for them to take action.

You need to be crystal clear of what benefits (not features) your product or service can provide the prospect with. Once you have identified these, you need to create an opening statement that clearly communicates these benefits in 10 to 15 seconds. I happen to train a couple of clients who sell PDQs and understand two major benefits their products offers are a big cost saving and, due to better connectivity, the ability to serve more customers and therefore do more business.

When the sales rep walks into a cafe, the first thing he/she does is find out who the owner is and then he she delivers the opening gambit that will go like this:

"I work for X company and have successfully been helping many cafes by significantly reducing their costs of their PDQs by over 40% and helping them serve more customers and therefore generating more business. I'm not sure if we can do the same for you, but to see if we can help you, can I ask what PDQ you have in place?"

The first thing to notice is the rep talked about success with other cafes like them, so it's important to use a relevant example i.e. a restaurant, a pub, a small retailer etc.

The rep used positive language like "successfully been helping", "significantly reducing" and "generating more business".

The rep only talked about the results he/she has helped other cafes achieve, as opposed to boring the prospect about himself or what he does.

The final point to note is what's called the take away phrase. The rep said, "I'm not sure if we can do the same for you, but to see if we can help you". This creates a desire as people want what they can't get. It's a great technique as you are not being too assumptive to say you can definitely help. However, you are forcing the owner to answer questions to see if they qualify in order for you to help them. Make sure you end with an open question that they cannot cut you off with; so in the rep's example, he said, "What PDQ do you have in place?" Once the rep had a reply, he/she would have followed up with a series of other planned questions regarding the connectivity, the service they receive from their supplier etc.

Tip 55

Dear Sales Doctor,

I normally try a prospect four times before giving up. Would you say that's about right or is there a set number you recommend?

That's a good question and there's not a set number really. To be successful in sales, you need to be tenacious and persistent. However, there is a very thin line between persistence and annoying the hell out of someone. You need to be 100% positive that you are chasing the right person, as the last thing you want to happen is you finally make contact and the person isn't the key decision maker for your product/service.

Once you have confirmed they are the right contact, I would suggest trying a variety of methods to make contact, such as telephone, email, handwritten letter, text or a gift of some kind i.e. a book that they would find of value. if your prospect is a financial director, they would probably appreciate a book on finance and you could write a handwritten note in the inside cover saying, "I hope you enjoy the book. I will be calling you over the next few days to discuss how I can help your business achieve a, b and c. look forward to speaking to you then."

In some instances, it can take up to six months to finally make contact. That does not mean you call them daily, otherwise you will definitely be stepping over that thin line. I would suggest three times the first week, twice the second and once the following week; then try every other week, leaving a space of a week or so in between. These days, you need to be creative to catch their attention and there are different ideas you could use, depending on the type of prospective customer they are. Here are a couple of ideals my clients have used and succeeded with:

I work with a courier company that targets blue-chip companies. They struggled getting hold of people so they sent chocolate feet on a stick in a branded box with a complimentary slip that read, "Now I have got my foot through the door, when is the best time for us to speak?" They received approximately 40% response rate and made an ROI on that direct mail by over 600%, so it was a wise move.

I train an opticians and they employ a couple of sales guys to call companies to organise eye tests. They were getting nowhere from cold calling and people were not returning their calls. They sent out a letter and the font size was six. Inside the envelope was a magnifying glass and the letter read, "If you can't read this letter without this magnifying glass, then you need your eyes tested." The salespeople then called all the companies that received the letter, and as you'd imagine, achieved an incredible response.

Both the above examples come with a cost; although minimal, it's still a cost none the less. So an example of something that costs very little is a client of mine sent an A4 envelope to their prospects and inside the envelope was a scrunched up piece of A4 paper. When the prospect opened the screwed up paper, it read, "This is the only thing we'll ever screw up...." Some people didn't respond well while others loved it; bottom line is some people were more receptive to taking their call.

Tip 56

Dear Sales Doctor,

I take both inbound calls and make outbound calls. Are there a certain set of questions you can recommend me using on a sales call?

It really does depend on the products and services you are selling and the average sales cycle you are working in. However, below are 15 great questions that I would recommend:

1.   Who recommended you to the Sales Doctor (your company name)?

This gets the source of the enquiry and gives the impression you receive many recommendations.

2.   When selecting a training partner, (insert your product/ service) what are the three most important things to you?

3.   Aside from yourself, who else needs to get involved in making the decision?

This identifies all decision makers that must be involved.

4.   What are your key objectives that you would like to receive as a result of doing business with me?

5.   Now I understand your objectives, please can you help me understand which are the three most important to you?

6.   Let's fast forward to six months' time; how will you know if working with me was a success?

This identifies the buyer's REAL objectives.

7. What is the decision making process within your organisation?

8. What time scales are you working towards?

9. What budget have you allocated for this project?

10. Which other companies have you spoken to about this project and what is your feedback on them compared to me so far?

11. What has prompted you to make this enquiry?

12. What are the biggest challenges within your sales team? (Insert the area your product/ service helps)

If making an outbound call:

13. If there were two areas you would change with your current supplier, what would they be?

14. When did you last review the market to ensure you are receiving the best quality product and service and paying the right price?

15. If your current supplier let you down or couldn't work within your time frames, who would you then go to in the market?

Tip 57

Dear Sales Doctor,

Sometimes I feel like a hamster in a wheel going around and around, doing the same thing. Most months I hit target (just) and I feel like the oomph has gone out of what I'm doing. How can I inject my next year with sales rejuvenation?

Sales is a funny game and I think you've used a great analogy to how many of us can feel in sales. The answer to your question will be different for each and every one of us. However, the same principle will apply for us all. It's all about what you want out of the selling that you do and what's the end result you have in mind.

I have asked all 3,000 salespeople that I have trained these three questions:

1. How many of you have set goals?
2. How many of you have written those goals down and put a deadline against each one?
3. How often do you go back and review those goals?

I would say around 10% of them actually set goals and out of those 300 or so people, only 50 of them have written the goals down; of which approximately 10 of whom have revisited their goals. With this in mind, it's no wonder the majority of us salespeople lose the oomph, as we have nothing to aim towards, no purpose.

I recently trained a sales recruitment company and one of the sales consultants said to me, "You are so passionate and enthusiastic about sales, Tony. I can never be like that." "Why do you think that is?" I asked him. He replied, "Sales doesn't interest me enough. I just can't seem to get energised about it." I explained to him the truth; I do not get passionate or energised about sales, I get enthused about the wonderful things that my success in sales brings me i.e. the lovely holidays with my family, the Porsche that I dreamt about as a young boy, my watch collection, the joy on my kids' faces when I buy them new toys etc. That's what ignites the flame in my belly, I explained. This really seemed to resonate with him and he has since written out a list of all his goals for the next 12 months and, most importantly, put a deadline next to each one.

The deadline is a really important part of the process, as it makes it real and creates urgency and is your way of committing to the goal. It's like if you book yourself on a marathon and have the date in your calendar; this motivates you to train as you have a clear goal that you are working towards.

Therefore, I would strongly recommend going away and writing out your goals for 2014. They don't have to be materialistic, it's whatever drives you; it could be a promotion in work, getting fit, learning a new subject, writing a book; the key is to write it down and put a date beside it. I find it helps to have pictures of your goals in front of you every day; this helps you focus on the things that are important to you and keeps you constantly motivated.

Please email me your goals on tony@wedosalestraining.com; once you have emailed them, it's a demonstration of your commitment to achieving them. I look forward to hearing from you.

Tip 58

Dear Sales Doctor,

I have just been promoted to a sales manager. Part of my role will be to recruit salespeople for my team. Are there key characteristics that I can look out for to assess if the person is right for sales?

Having been fortunate to train over 3,000 sales professionals, you do get to really understand what makes a top performing sales professional and conversely what are the biggest failures of a salesperson.

Characteristics of an outstanding sales professional:

- They set goals in writing
- They are self-disciplined
- They are self-motivated
- They want to learn and gain new knowledge
- They like building relationships
- They are enthusiastic
- They are observant and always spotting opportunities
- They are self-confident
- They love people
- They like themselves; comfortable in their own skin
- They thrive on a challenge
- They absolutely love to win
- They can accept rejection with a positive attitude (ask how they view failure; the perfect answer is they view it as feedback)

- They are good on detail

- They are skilled communicators

- They are hard workers

- They are tenacious

Characteristics of an under-performing salesperson, with some tips to prove them:

- They are subservient; bordering on desperation, they will do anything the prospect asks, just to win their business
  - The key here is to only agree to give something, if you get something back in return i.e. if I drop the price, I want a testimonial or a referral

- The salesperson talks at them and goes into feature bash mode, as opposed to asking some well prepared questions to get the prospect talking

- They often mistakenly think a verbal agreement is a deal done
  - It's important to write everything that is agreed down and repeat back to the prospect that has been agreed

- Poor salespeople often speak badly about the competition
  - A better suggestion is to say "my worth competitor" or explain why your clients feel you are more superior

- They make follow-up calls by saying, "I'm just calling to see if you received my brochure?"
  - I would recommend providing value and suggestions for the prospect

- Many poor salespeople try and overcome objections with words
  - Much better overcoming a prospect's objections with testimonials

- Many salespeople are just focusing on getting the sale; as opposed to trying to build rapport and make the prospect like them

- Underperformed salespeople make 'fluffy verbal agreements' about the next steps
    - Much better to organise a firm appointment for a second meeting to a follow-up call in the diary

- Not doing what you promised you would

- Not listening properly

- Giving the price, before the prospect has asked for it

- Thinking you're smarter than the prospect

- MOST IMPORTANTLY – asking for the business

"Questions are
never indiscreet,
answers
sometimes are."

Oscar Wilde

Tip 59

Dear Sales Doctor,

I have recently joined an estate agent in South London as a lettings negotiator and have no experience. We have been told to find our own properties, but have been given no guidance or ideas. Can you help?

This is probably the biggest challenge that my estate agency clients currently face and where I have been able to provide the most help and value, so you're in luck!

The first thing you need to do is generate landlords' details and then you need to learn how to call them to win the valuation, which will then hopefully turn into an instruction. So let's start with gaining the landlords' details.

There are three main sources I recommend for this. Firstly, every applicant that walks into your branch, calls up your branch or emails your branch, could be a potential source of landlord leads. As you are qualifying them, you need to find out where they are currently living; ask yourself, is this in our catchment area? If so, are they renting or do they own the property? If they own the property, you need to ask them what they plan on doing with the property and if they are planning to sell, then you must arrange a valuation.

If they are currently renting and the property falls within your catchment area, then I would recommend the following pitch:

"As I'm sure you know, Mr Applicant, the rental market is currently moving extremely fast; we can take a property on and within three hours, it's let. Therefore, I need to do a very quick reference on you, to make sure you have been a good tenant. Can I just take your landlord's details please?

Now, not all the applicants will know their landlord's details, as they only deal with the agency they rented the property through. Secondly, not all applicants will be willing to provide their landlord's details; however, some will and if you don't ask, you don't get. To reassure you, one of the biggest estate agents in London, with over 40 branches, has set up new departments to concentrate solely on this.

The second source of landlords' details are Gumtree and Loot. You will see numerous adverts on properties to let, that clearly states no estate agents. However, dealt with the right way, this can be extremely fruitful in winning valuations.

Thirdly, if no other negotiator has taken the initiative to do this already, speak to the Head of Property Management or the owners of your agency and recommend calling your existing landlords. The objective of the call is to ask for referrals of any other landlords they know or other properties they have may have to let; however, I would start the call as a courtesy call to ensure they have been happy with the service they have received.

How do we call the landlord to win the valuation?

This is my recommendation for how we call the landlords that we gained from applicants, our first source of landlords leads.

"Good morning, John. Thanks for taking my call. My name is Tony Morris, calling from X agency. Your tenant, John Smith, has just left our agency and I wanted to do a very quick reference on him.

Has he been a good tenant?
Did he pay his bills on time?
Did he look after your property?

"That's great, thanks for that. I noticed your property falls in the middle of our catchment area, where we have been renting properties for the past 25 years. How are you currently marketing your property?"

Ask a few more questions to show an interest and then arrange a valuation.

The second call is the landlords from Gumtree or Loot. Look up the specific property on Google Street maps, so you know exactly where the property is situated. It's possible you have let property in roads nearby. If so, this is worth mentioning as it builds your credibility as an agent.

"Good morning, John. Thanks for taking my call. My name is Tony Morris. Is your property on Bedford Hill still available?

"Great, how flexible are you on the rent?

Can you tell me a bit more about the property? How near is it to the station? What is the size of the second room? Is there a garden?

"Fantastic! I have three professionally vetted tenants desperate for what you have just described. If I can get you £850 per month after our fees, you would be happy with that, wouldn't you?"

You need to run this suggestion past the owners of your agency, to get their consent. They need to agree with the fee structure I have recommended, as this may not suit their business. What I am saying is, the landlord needs £850 per month as an example, but if we can achieve £950 month, then we get paid £1,200 a year and the landlord gets his rent, so everyone is happy.

If the landlord starts to object, a good question to ask him./her is, "Why are you only asking £850 per month for it?" (Give the impression you think you can achieve more.)

Finally ask him/her when the best time for viewings is, morning or afternoons.

The third and final call is landlords from your existing landlords. This is by far the easiest of all the calls. If possible, dependent on your relationship with the existing landlord, you could ask them to send an email or even better, make a quick introductory call, to let the landlord know you will be calling and put in a good word. When making the call, I would suggest the following words:

"Good morning, Mr Landlord. Thanks for taking my call. My name is Tony Morris, calling from X Agency. I have kindly been given your details from John Smith, whom we have been successfully looking after his property for X years. The reason for my call is to discuss the possibility of helping look after your property as well. Can I ask, how are you currently marketing your property?"

Tip 60

Dear Sales Doctor,

My boss keeps telling me I'm puking over my prospects when I'm cold calling them about our commercial utilities offer, but won't give me any help and guidance. Any ideas would be massively appreciated?

This call may resonate with you in that case. I got a call the other day from a salesman selling printers and photocopiers and it was painful to say the least. It went like this:

Salesman: Good morning, Tony. It's John Smith from ABC Printers. Is it a convenient time to speak?

Me: What's it regarding?

Salesman: What it is, we are currently calling around all companies based in London to find out what printers and photocopiers they have in place, their ink usage and the maintenance contracts they have in place with their current suppliers and seeing if there is anything we can do to save them money. We are one of the leading companies in the market and have won awards for the quality of our printers...

(At this point, I am losing the will for HIM to live; however, it continues.....)

......and service levels and work with numerous blue-chips corporations all over London providing them with our blah blah printers and photocopiers. They love the fact we offer a PMS system [I later found out from Google this stands for a print management service] which tells us when their ink is running low and we order it for them automatically. We are based in Reading and was wondering if you would be interested in having an appointment with one of my sales reps to discuss your current printing and photocopier contract?

I wish this call was made up. However, it was one of the most painful, yet common sales calls I hear people make again and again, and they wonder why they don't achieve any results. I label this call 'the salesman's puke', for the simple fact they do not let the prospect get a word in edgeways and they just puke all over them and hope someone will say yes. The truth is, some do say yes; however, that's probably to get the irritating salesman off the phone and to stop puking over them.

So how should a sales call like this be done? The key is to engage the prospect and give value and to get the prospect talking. In this day and age, no one likes being sold to; however, people do like to buy. We can only get people to buy from us if we know what they want and need, and only then are we in a position to recommend them something. So my suggestion would be along these lines:

Salesman: Good morning, Tony. It's John Smith from ABC Printers. Thanks for taking my call. Are you familiar with my business?

Me: No, I haven't heard of you. What's this regarding?

Salesman: We have successfully helped many sales training companies, like you, by reducing their printing and photocopiers costs and offering exceptional ongoing maintenance support. To see if we can help you as well, can I ask what are your current printing and photocopier requirements?

If we analyse this opening statement, I have made it harder for the prospect to stop the call by not asking if it's convenient to speak. I have told the prospect very quickly what's in it for him by explaining how we have helped companies like his.

Rather than give the impression I am calling a long list of companies in London and you are my 77th call, I have specified the industry I have had major success in (sales training companies) to demonstrate I have done my homework before making the call.

Finally, I have engaged the prospect by asking a good open question which will get him/her speaking. Then based on the information I would have gained, would have allowed me to recommend one of my experts (sales reps) to have a free consultation to see exactly how we can help him.

So before puking all over the prospect, think about whom you are calling and what value you can bring to their business and then plan your opening statement and questions to ask. Then make a great sales call.

"We are all in the business of sales. Teachers sell students on learning, parents sell their children on making good grades and behaving, and traditional salesmen sell their products."

Dave Ramsey

"Time is the coin of your life.
It is the only coin you have,
and only you can determine
how it will be spent.
Be careful lest you
let other people
spend it for you."

Carl Sandburg

Tip 61

Dear Sales Doctor,

I work in publishing and there is often friction between the sales and editorial/design teams. I need to concentrate on selling while they need me to help with admin/client chasing. How do you propose I juggle both?

It's a very common challenge we have as salespeople, to be pulled from pillar to post. My initial response to this question is to ask, "Is there other resources within the business that you could delegate this work to?"

The reason I ask that is for this simple point, what is your time worth? As a sales trainer and speaker, I charge my clients by the day and therefore am able to calculate what I'm worth by the hour; which is approximately £250 per hour. Therefore you could argue, would it not be better for me to hire someone and pay them £10 an hour, rather than do it myself?

All the time you are chasing clients for money and dealing with administration, is time you are NOT focusing on generating new business from prospective customers or from your existing client base. Please bear in mind this is not a conversation you have with the person in editorial and design, as inevitably they will be extremely defensive and it will add fuel to the flame.

My recommendation would be to speak to the person whose overall responsibility it is in the business to bring in the sales figures; probably your sales director or MD. They may agree with my view about what you are worth and take the commercial decision to delegate the admin and credit chasing to somebody else.

If, on the other hand, they disagree, and you are told that admin and client chasing is part of your job, then you need to manage that differently.

As a sales professional, there are certain times of the day that are most effective to be making sales calls i.e. 09:30am to 12:30 and 13:30 to 17:00. Therefore, if possible, I would use all the other time available to carry out the admin and client chasing duties. I appreciate this is not always possible; so if your role involves you travelling by train, use this time to carry out those tasks as well; it's a case of working smarter, not harder.

Equally when client chasing, use those calls to achieve other objectives. When I speak to clients, I am looking to develop my relationship with them, generate new business opportunities within their business, ask for a testimonial and gain referrals from them; who better to ask for a referral than a happy customer?

Tip 62

Dear Sales Doctor,

We are trying to recruit more salespeople to build our team. We are an SME and don't have a formal HR department; we also don't have the money to pay big recruitment fees. Can you give us any advice on recruiting the right people on a limited budget?

Finding good salespeople is extremely challenging, especially with a proven track record of success. The most important characteristic to look out for when meeting candidates is a genuine positive attitude. This is not sometime that can be taught and is quite rare to find, however, skills can be taught and practices developed.

Now, where to find them?

As you're on a budget, recruitment companies are not going to be an option for you. If their fee is that low that it becomes affordable, then you could probably do as good a job as they'll do.

I would recommend being crystal clear on the type of salesperson you are looking for and then write a job description and job advert. To get assistance on this, just look at some written on job boards such as Jobsite. co.uk and Reed.co.uk; that will provide plenty of choice to help you.

Once you are satisfied that you've written the right job advert and description, post it on the job boards. I would recommend Gumtree as this is £30 for the month and can be very successful. Depending on your budget, either try this for a week and see the response you get or post it on one of the top job boards. I've had the best response form Reed in the past when looking for salespeople.

Now here is a couple of great tips.

On the advert, use a phone number that goes directly to a voicemail that you have set up. The voice message should clearly welcome them to the recruitment line and ask the candidate to leave their name and number and, in a couple of sentences, why they feel they are right for the job. As a good telephone manner is an important part of sales, this idea will immediately screen out about 40% of candidates.

You then call back the approximately 40% of candidates to politely tell them they haven't been successful and to thank them for applying.

With the remaining 60% of candidates, call them back and organise a telephone interview for that afternoon.

Provide them with a time slot and separate these by 15 minute intervals. Again, approximately 30% of the candidates will not be bothered to call back, which separates the wheat from the chaff. These two screening processes remove the time wasters and allows you to invest your time with the right people.

After you've carried out your 15 minute telephone interview, invite the successful candidates to a first stage face-to-face interview. Just before you invite them, say, "We have been inundated for this job. If you would like to go away and think about it, that's absolutely fine; just let me know what you'd like to do." Now only a small percent like to think about it; however, again, it's another process to remove the ones that are not fully committed.

Then hold your interviews and choose who impresses you most. Some key things to look out for in a successful sales candidate are:

1. Their appearance - have they dressed the part?

2. Ask them a few things about your company - if they haven't done their homework, they are not that committed.

3.   Have they prepared some questions to ask you about your company and the job? This demonstrates how interested they are.

4.   Do they close you at the end by saying something along the lines of "What is the next step? Do you think I'll fit in with your company? Can I have the job?"

5.   And my favourite question - "Do you have any reservations at all about me, which I can clear up now, that could prevent me from going through to the next stage?"

Best of luck on finding your team and if you need any help, please get in touch at tony@wedosalestraining.com

Once you've recruited, don't forget to call me to organise sales training!

"In my experience,
there is only one motivation,
and that is desire.
No reasons or principle
contain it or
stand against it."

Jane Smiley

Tip 63

Dear Sales Doctor,

I really struggle to be self-motivated. Are you aware of any practical ways that I can motivate myself on a daily basis?

I don't know if you are a football fan, but when the manager gives his motivational pep talk, where do you think he delivers it? In the trophy room, but why? Because he wants the team to be surrounded by success. So my first suggestion is to keep track of every sale you make in a book or an excel spreadsheet and refer back to it regularly to keep reminding yourself of how good you are.

Set goals. Every salesperson should be goal orientated. However, they don't have to be financial. Your goal could be to become a sales manager, to beat your previous month's sales figures etc. The point is to set a goal and make sure they are SMART - Specific, Measurable, Achievable, Realistic and Timely. A goal without these are just dreams. I find setting mini goals every day or every week are very motivational i.e. this week I'm going to ask three clients for a recommendation. By setting the goal, you are far more motivated to making it happen.

Get yourself into a positive mindset. The way you achieve this must be personal to you; for example, I wake up 20 minutes earlier than I need to so that I can spend that invaluable time with my kids. This always gets me into a good and positive mindset. Other suggestions are to do some brief exercises, go for a walk, watch an episode of your favourite comedy show. Make sure you avoid negative people; they'll drain all your positive energy.

Always look for feedback. The beauty of sales is there is no such thing as failure; it's all feedback. Always go back to your client or prospect and ask what you could have done differently to be successful.

I normally write an email and make it clear that they will not offend me and I want their honest and valued feedback as I'm always looking to develop and improve. I feel that by asking this in an email, it allows people to be honest and not get embarrassed about providing constructive feedback. Remember, every lesson you take away from a sales situation will arm you better for your next encounter.

Set yourself personal challenges. Similar to goal setting, make sure you are always striving to better yourself and making small improvements. Whenever I go to the gym, I always try and run one metre more in the 10 minutes. This forces me to push myself every time.

My final suggestion is to remember to congratulate and reward yourself. Many salespeople I train do achieve great things and then are immediately thinking of their next challenge. It's important to remember to take some time out and reward your success. This could be buying yourself a well deserved gift, eating out somewhere nice, having a little break etc.

Tip 64

Dear Sales Doctor,

I'm good at sales, but I'm finding it hard leaving my home stress at the door. It's affecting my working life. Have you got any advice on how to focus?

This is extremely common and very challenging. In one way or another, everyone has home stress, some unfortunately worse than others. I think the initial thing to appreciate is everyone has home stress and you are not alone. It's part of life and it must be viewed the same as when we get rejected in sales; it's part of the process. If we allowed every sales knock-back to affect us, we would never pick up the phone or attend a sales meeting again.

People handle home stress differently; I like to work out and go to the gym and take the stress out by doing a great work out or go for a jog - I find the fresh air and the cardio really helps. Other people like to soak in a bath, read a book and take their mind off things.

The lesson here is to do something, take action and try different things and see what works best for you. What many people do is focus on the home stress and worry about it, which of course only magnifies the problem and does the opposite to helping you handle it better.

I suppose you could compare this to challenges that every entrepreneur faces in their business. The way they handle and overcome the challenge is the true strength of an entrepreneur, as opposed to stressing and worrying about it; they view it as an inevitable part of the process and learn how to handle it head on.

Tony Morris

I guarantee every successful entrepreneur has experienced their fair share of home stress; it's just they learned how to handle it as part of everyday life.

Don't be scared of asking for support outside of your home, as I am sure there are people who would be only too happy to help; many people feel it's rude to ask.

"In business, you're the Chief Salesman. Create a sense of demand, rather than waiting to have demand."

Barbara Corcoran

Tip 65

Dear Sales Doctor,

I sell skip hire door to door and I'm finding most receptionists are saying it's a no name policy and are not willing to get the right person to come and see me, or provide me with the person's contact details. I'm starting to think it is best to cold call on the phone; however, I really need advice. Please help.

Your comments are very common and companies are getting tougher and tougher at blocking cold callers at the door.

Therefore, it's crucial to be more targeted and know the decision maker's name when you walk in and say, "I'm here to see X. I'm a little early as we arranged a meeting at 11am and it's 10:45am."

Best way, X comes downs and acts confused and you explain you arranged it with their colleague and you can't recall their name. They would normally give you 10 minutes just out of courtesy.

Worst way, X is not present and the receptionist will feel obliged to help and get X's colleague to come downstairs to try and help. You can then qualify that person to understand the situation regarding skips and waste management.

I do agree with your comments and feel telemarketing is a more effective way to spend your time.

The only time I suggest cold door knocking is once a meeting has been made and you knock doors in and around where the meeting is; remembering to get the decision maker's name as suggested above.

There is free websites to get data, like www.businessmagnet.com and www.ufindus.com, and there are many list brokers if you want to pay for more targeted data. You need to identify your ideal customer and create a hit list and then the broker can quote how many leads they have that fits.

"There's no lotion or potion
that will make sales faster
and easier for you -
unless your potion
is hard work."

Jeffrey Gitomer

Tip 66

Dear Sales Doctor,

I'd like to show my sales team how important they are to the business. Have you any advice about incentives?

I have some great incentive ideas that my clients use for their sales team; but what's important to find out first is what would incentivise your sales team? Without knowing this, it's very difficult to incentivise your people. In my opinion, this is the responsibility of the sales manager to know exactly what motivates and demotives each person in his/her sales team.

I have a client who runs a 150 seat call centre of telemarketers and they do daily competitions where people can win a bottle of wine, a box of chocolates, a duvet day (come into work late) and many more prizes. What transpired after doing a survey with all the staff, is the incentive the majority valued the most is the £10 trophy that was given out on close of play on Friday for the performer of the week. You would never have guessed that people actually cared about this little trophy; however, the call centre manager used to get people knocking his door down at 18:00 on a Friday asking where their trophy was.

When choosing the right incentives for your team, you have to consider the sort of environment and culture you would like on your sales floor. If you want a loud and exciting sales floor, then I would recommend a points system which I call a sales ladder. You decide on a list of categories that you would like to incentivise your team to achieve, as it's important to not just reward the top sales performer, otherwise people will start to resent that person and give up in the month when they realise they can't win. On the following page is an idea of categories that an IT hardware client of mine uses:

- Most calls made in the week

- Most amount of proactive referrals gained in the week

- Most meetings made in the week

- Most quotes sent out in the week

- Most business closed in the week

- Highest deal closed in the week

- Most testimonials received in the week

- Hardest worker of the week – manager's discretion

You need to allocate points to each category i.e. each could be worth 10 points and you then decide the value of a point i.e. 1 point = £1. Only one person can win per category, therefore it incentivises the team to compete to try and beat their peers. You can have a big whiteboard up in your office with a list of all the categories down the left hand side and the names of the sales team at the top; this way, they can personally enter their figures on the board at close of play every day and take ownership i.e. if John Smith makes most meetings in the day, he will enter a star by his name that day. At the end of the week, they count up to see who gets awarded the points.

Many of my clients insist the sales team have to accrue their points for a minimum of three months before cashing them in. They are allowed to gamble them at the end of the month if they wish i.e. double or nothing and you can put a dartboard in the office; again, this all depends on what environment you want on your sales floor.

As most salespeople are incentivised by commission, I would suggest they have to cash the points in for prizes, worth the value of the points. This allows the salesperson to choose the gift that they feel is an incentive. I've had clients where the guys choose to drive a Ferrari for the weekend and the ladies choose a day in a spa. The beauty of this sales ladder is it works as a great incentive, and creates and encourages healthy competition in the office.

One final thought to add to the sales ladder is to have a plaque in the office saying 'Top Sales Performer of the Month' with a framed picture of the salesperson above it. You can use the sales who achieve the most points in the month, or this could be for the person who brings in the most revenue; again, this needs to be decided by management.

If that idea appeals and you have the right environment, it's always good to have a trophy for the top performer that you give out every three or six months. They could win 100 points when they receive the trophy.

One of the best ways to incentivise a sales team is team building days. At my company, Sales Doctor, we run a fantastic team building day called 'The Apprentice Day'. It's ideal for sales teams with between 8 and 20 staff and we set 20 activities for the two teams to carry out in the day in London or their nearest city centre location.

The feedback we receive is incredible and our clients love the fact it allows the team to practise all their sales skills from negotiation, cold calling, leadership, planning etc. in a fun packed day. To find out more, please email me on tony@wedosalestraining.com and write 'The Apprentice Day' in the subject line.

Conclusion

Successful sales is down to two areas - skills and attitude.

Attitude is something that can't be taught; you can't teach someone to have a positive attitude. You can make them think about what actually motivates them, but it's up to them to act on those things.

The word motivation is derived from the Latin term motivus ("a moving cause"), it's the forces acting either on or within a person to initiate behaviour. As the definition suggests, it's up to THE person to initiate the behaviour.

The wonderful part of sales to me is you never stop learning. There is a constant flow of new skills, words, techniques and ideas that are always available to us; it's just our choice of whether we choose to act on them.

I hope this book has given you some ideas and techniques on how to handle some challenging situations. The key is to keep going back and refreshing yourself so they become second nature.

One major element that separates the wheat from the chaff when it comes to sales is organisation. It's imperative to have a system that works for you, to ensure you ALWAYS follow up and stay on top of every prospect. Most salespeople I train fall down in this area, which is such a shame as you do all the work to create the opportunity and build value about your offering. Therefore, staying on top of them should be the easy part.

As a sales trainer, I am always keen to help develop sales professionals. Please email me on tony@wedosalestraining.com with any questions you have about your particular sales role that I haven't answered in my book; I'd be only too happy to help.

Tony Morris

I ask only two things of you in return. Firstly, if you have enjoyed this book, please be so kind to write a brief review on Amazon sharing your thoughts and opinions on how you have benefited from this book. If you didn't enjoy the book, then write nothing and keep it to yourself!

Secondly, if there is anyone you know in the sales world that you feel would also benefit from my book, then kindly email them about it.

Please keep me updated on your success; I'd love to hear your stories.

Join my LinkedIn group, Sales Doctor Q&A and ask me your most challenging sales questions, and I and the other members will provide great practical answers to help you.

Now go out and be the best sales professional you can be, every day!

This is my prescription for you!

The Sales Doctor

About the Sales Doctor

www.wedosalestraining.com

Sales Doctor delivers 100% bespoke training courses around your business and team's needs. We have a unique four stage approach to tailor every course we deliver:

Stage 1

A one day diagnosis

At Sales Doctor, we like to diagnose our delegates before training them and making them better. We listen to them on the phone and have a one-to-one with them to discuss areas they want the training to include, understanding their individual challenges and specific areas they wish to grow and develop. This allows us to develop a bespoke training course based on the business's requirements and what we have learned.

The mystery calls

Before training, we provide mystery calls, so we can test the techniques that are being used prior to training. These allow us to gain a true insight into what the team are doing well and areas that need development and truly tailor the training accordingly. All calls are recorded and we use them in training as a session for the team to listen to and provide constructive feedback.

Stage 2

The training course

This is always tailored around our clients' needs and the number of days is based upon their specific requirements.

Stage 3

The one day check up

This is where we return to the client approximately one to two weeks after training to refresh them and discuss what has and hasn't worked. We then tweak certain areas and ensure all the delegates have a clear focus on the areas they will be working on.

Stage 4

The open clinic

At Sales Doctor, we run an open clinic, which allows your team to have access via phone or email to me or one of my co-directors to help ensure that everything we have done is reinforced, and provide comfort for those who feel they need it e.g. before they meet a prospective client and just want to discuss their agenda. This is unique in our industry and we pride ourselves on its benefit and success. **This is ongoing as some delegates need a little bit longer to become exceptional and therefore we do not put any time limit on this whatsoever.**

We are salespeople who train, as opposed to trainers who lecture. Therefore, we can empathise with your team and can give real-life examples to their problems, rather than theory which are impossible to put into practice. All our training is fun, participative and interactive. Your team will walk away enthused to pick up the phone and start putting the new techniques straight into practice.

Whether your team have 20 years of sales experience or are brand new to the field, we can tailor a course around them. We carry out role plays and group exercises throughout training and where we see fit we make live calls to real prospects to enable your team to practise their new skills and techniques.

We deliver bespoke sales training courses to include:

- Telephone sales (inbound and outbound)
- Field sales
- Account Management

We deliver bespoke sales management courses which is focused on the real life of managing sales teams and provides practical ideas to get the best from your sales team.

Whether your team sells over the phone, face-to-face or is involved in presentations, we will have a course that is right for you. All our trainers have over 15 years' of experience, in selling, managing salespeople and training. With over 270 clients in over 70 industries, we have a wealth of experience that we can bring to the table to add value to your business.

We are proud to have worked with Oakley sunglasses, Wren Kitchens and bedrooms, Polypipe and many more great companies.